NOA

MADELEINES IN MANHATTAN

MADELEINES IN MANHATTAN

A MEMOIR WITH RECIPES

COLETTE ROSSANT

ISIS
LARGE PRINT
Oxford

First published in Great Britain 2007
by
Bloomsbury Publishing Plc

Published in Large Print 2007 by ISIS Publishing Ltd.,
7 Centremead, Osney Mead, Oxford OX2 0ES
by arrangement with
Bloomsbury Publishing Plc

British Library Cataloguing in Publication Data
Rossant, Colette
   Madeleines in Manhattan: a memoir with
recipes. – Large print ed.
   1. Rossant, Colette
   2. French – New York (State) – New
      York – Biography
   3. Cookery, American
   4. Large type books
   5. New York (N.Y.) – Social life and customs
      – 20th century
   I. Title
   974.7'1'043'092

ISBN 978–0–7531–9442–3 (hb)
ISBN 978–0–7531–9443–0 (pb)

Printed and bound in Great Britain by
T. J. International Ltd., Padstow, Cornwall

To my children and grandchildren

When they were wild
When they were not yet human
When they could be anything
I was on the other side with milk to lure them
And their father, too, each name a net in his hand

Birth by Louise Erdrich

CONTENTS

ACKNOWLEDGEMENTS

Over the past few years, many people have helped me through difficult times. I want to thank the Bogliasco Foundation who offered me a haven of peace and quiet to write this book; my friend Rosemary Ahern for her editorial help and suggestions; my very good friend and agent Gloria Loomis for believing in me; Peter Borland, my editor at Atria, who has beautifully edited this book; at Bloomsbury Alexandra Pringle for her patience with me and Chiki Sarkar for her enthusiasm and her support. Finally I thank my husband Jimmy, without whom this book would never have been written.

CHAPTER
ONE

The Move

We are on our way to Le Havre. The train is going so fast that the landscape is all but a blur. From time to time I can see a farm in the mist surrounded by a sea of green fields. I am excited, but also scared. It is 1955 and we are on our way to New York. Jimmy and I were married a couple of months ago. The week before our wedding Anne, my mother-in-law, and my mother fought all the time: two jealous women bickering about dresses, jewellery, food, me, and God knows what else. They were horrible, like two witches. They nearly ruined my wedding. But as usual Mira, my stepfather, saved the day. Mira, born in Normandy, believed that food, that is, very good food, could solve any problem. He took Anne to lunch in a two-star restaurant. She loved it. Back home, she talked lovingly about eating snails with Swiss chard.

"I had a great lunch! Snails with Swiss chard? I've never had that before. I simply *loved* it," she had said, smiling happily for the first time in weeks. My mother looked slightly miffed.

1

"Well Anne, I'm *so* happy you liked it. Mira *does* know the best restaurants. Maybe tomorrow you and I can try La Coupole?"

"Yes, of course! But only if you let *me* take *you* out for lunch."

From that day on, my mother and Anne had a truce that lasted until the day of the wedding.

Anne's choice of dress for the wedding, pale green tulle, was shocking to my conservative mother. "Can you imagine? At her age! Wearing a young ballerina's dress!" my mother had whispered to her best friend on the telephone a few days earlier, recounting all the real or imagined problems she had with my future mother-in-law. My stepfather once again saved the day by taking them both out to dinner at Potin on Avenue Victor Hugo, with the excuse that they should try the food as Potin were catering the reception. "Anne loves sole," he had whispered to me. "They make the best sole in Paris." He was right. The two women both chose and devoured the *sole meunière*.

The next few days were calm despite the problems I had with my brother and my grandmother. My brother, who was doing his military service in Algeria, had refused to come to my wedding on the grounds that Jimmy was an American and therefore not well educated.

"Marry a Frenchman," he had written, "not an American. He does not belong in our family."

I did not get along with him since he resented me invading his space when I came back from Egypt in 1947.

2

My French grandmother, who also objected to my marrying Jimmy rather than the young man of her choice, had refused to attend the wedding and had left the country for the States to visit old friends.

I had loved my grandfather. Although he had died just before we came back to Paris, I remembered him quite well as we had lived in Paris till I was six years old. We left for Egypt in 1939 when my father became quite ill, and my Egyptian grandfather, thinking that the hot Egyptian climate would help him get better, summoned us to Cairo. My brother disliked Cairo, the heat, the noise and above all seeing my father ill and helpless. I was too young and did not realize how seriously ill he was. Within a few weeks of our arrival in Cairo, my brother, who was then ten years old, wanted to go back to Paris. My parents, ill advised, and despite the rumours of an impending war, sent my brother back alone to France to live with my French grandparents. I would not see my brother again until I was fourteen.

My father died a year later. My mother, now a thirty-year-old widow, decided that she needed to find herself, to seek a new life and a new husband. A young child, she felt, would hamper her progress; she decided that I would live with my Egyptian grandparents and for the next five years I never saw or heard from her.

We were an extended Jewish Sephardic family. We all lived in an enormous house near the Nile, in the posh neighbourhood of Garden City. My grandparents, their two grown daughters and I lived on the first floor. My grandparent's oldest son, his wife and five children

3

lived on the second floor. On the third and fourth floor lived two of his other children with their wives and children.

The family was large (my grandmother had had nine children), boisterous and loving. Being the youngest of all the children and treated by everyone as an orphan, I was looked after by uncles, aunts and older cousins. I had the run of the house, but my favourite hiding place was the kitchen. I loved the warmth of the kitchen. It is there that I fell in love with food and Ahmet, the cook who treated me like his own child.

When I was fourteen my mother reappeared and insisted that I return to Paris to further my education. I was heartbroken to leave my Egyptian family, especially when my mother, once in Paris, left me with her mother, a paragon of rectitude. Mother once again disappeared, for another three years.

My French grandmother disliked me intensely for several reasons: first for having, like my mother, converted to Catholicism; secondly for speaking French with an Egyptian accent; and finally for not being elegant. Furthermore, she felt I was unsettling the close-knit circle consisting of herself and my brother (my grandfather had died at the end of the war). I was having quite a miserable time, trying to woo my grandmother and my brother who ignored me; trying to lose my Egyptian accent and learn to become a Parisian. I failed in the first, but lost my Egyptian accent. As for becoming a real Parisian, the task was too tough as I was short, plump and had no one to teach me how to dress and be elegant.

Jimmy and I had met in 1949, when I was sixteen. Anne had offered Jimmy a trip to Europe after his graduation. She had met my grandparents before the war and they had remained good friends; she had given him their address in Paris in case he ran out of money, which he did. To a sixteen-year-old teenager this young twenty-year-old, tall, handsome American was a dream come true. We fell in love and to my mother's dismay I announced that I wanted to marry him right away. My mother, who for years had not paid any attention to me, suddenly became very involved. I cried, got angry, but I could do nothing to change her mind. She kept on repeating the same thing over and over:

"Ridiculous! You are too young, you are still in high school. He has to go back to school and choose a profession. No more talk about that."

Her mother, for the first time, agreed with her. Then finally to stop the argument my mother said that if in five years we still felt the same we could get married.

Jimmy and I swore that we would wait. He promised to come back for me. We corresponded from time to time and five years later, as promised, he reappeared in my life. Jimmy was then doing his military service and was stationed in Munich. To the horror of my family, especially my grandmother, I joined him there and we lived together for a year until we were able to get married. Jimmy was in the intelligence corps and getting permission to marry to a foreigner while in the service took a whole year. We were finally married on 8 September 1955. The wedding was lovely; the reception at Potin went well, even if a former boyfriend Francis, angry that I had turned him down and also drunk, threw a glass of champagne into Jimmy's face. Everyone laughed. The rest of the evening was more peaceful. After the wedding we went back to Germany. Jimmy had another nine months to serve. He was discharged in Munich and together we went to live and work in Italy. By the end of 1956, Jimmy felt it was time to return to New York and start a new life there as an architect, and also as a family.

We went to Paris to say our goodbyes. On our last Sunday Mira suggested that Jimmy and I go to the Boulevard Raspail market to buy food for lunch and dinner. As we walked through the market, the smells were overwhelming. Jimmy wanted to buy everything. We stopped in front of an asparagus stand. The first asparagus of the season: fat white asparagus with purple tops next to bunches of pale green wild asparagus that looked more like ferns. We bought some of each. Then we stopped at a charcuterie stand and bought some *pâté de campagne*, duck *rillettes* and *boudins noirs* (blood sausages). We bought two pounds of cherries and I ate half of them as we continued our walk. The cheese stand was our next stop. There I bought a *chèvre*, and a piece of Cantal and Mira's favourite cheese, a ripe Roblochon. Just before leaving the market I picked up crusty country bread and a dozen farm fresh eggs.

Back at home I showed Mira our purchases. Jimmy was hovering over us saying he was starving and wanted lunch. Mira and I decided to make asparagus with boiled eggs, one of Mira's specialities. We agreed that we would start with the white asparagus, then serve the *boudin* with mashed potatoes, and prepare the wild asparagus with mushrooms for dinner. As we peeled the asparagus, Mira handed me one to eat raw. Crunchy and delicious, with a taste of freshly cut grass.

Once cooked, I placed some asparagus on each plate with a boiled egg and clarified butter. I had to explain to Jimmy how to eat them.

"Pour a tablespoon of melted butter into the egg, add salt and pepper and mix it with a spoon, then dip the asparagus into the egg."

We all laughed when Jimmy picked up his knife and fork to eat the asparagus. In France, I explained to him, you don't cut asparagus, you pick it up with your fingers and eat it, sucking the stalks. The light, creamy taste of the egg yolk enhances the soft, earthy taste of the asparagus. Mira said that sometimes he would add some truffle juice, but that he had none that day. For dinner we steamed the wild asparagus, sautéed the mushrooms and served the asparagus topped with the mushrooms.

Jimmy smiled. "Delicious, I never tasted something so light and fresh. I don't want to leave Paris!" We both looked at him.

"Are you serious?" I asked.

"No. I do want to go back. New York is where I belong. But I *will* miss this sensational food."

The next day we left for New York. We were sailing on the *Liberté*, once a German liner leftover from the war and now totally refurbished and renamed. Mira had pulled some strings and we were given a first-class state-room. Remembering how ill I had been on the passage from Egypt to Marseilles on our return to France years before, my mother produced pills for seasickness. I hoped I would not need them. My mother swore that this new medicine would help. For the last three weeks she had been very solicitous, even overbearing. I was not used to it. Normally she would have nothing to do with me. Now she dragged me through stores to shop for a trousseau I insisted I did not need.

"I don't want to go shopping. I don't need anything."

"Yes you do. You cannot go to New York without nice sheets and some tablecloths. You need towels and . . ."

Resistance, I realized, was futile. I gave in.

We bought towels, sheets with my initials, pillowcases and tablecloths. My wedding presents had included fifteen tea tablecloths. "I don't invite friends for tea," I told my mother, who obliged me to keep at least two. The fancy silver went back to the stores: Jimmy hated it. We kept the china and the glasses, a gift from Murray, Jimmy's brother. They had been sent to America. My mother and I bought dresses, a coat, shoes and handbags. I didn't understand why my mother, who has never bought me anything, thought it so important that I would be well dressed and have sheets with my initials. Who would see my bed? I was sure Jimmy did not care, but I went along with her wishes. At my stepfather's suggestion, she bought

8

enormous wicker baskets to pack everything in. Simpler to send, he explained to me. I think that perhaps she was happy to finally get rid of me.

Jimmy urged me to be more patient and kinder to my mother.

"I can't. She never took care of me! Why now? I can't erase twenty years of neglect." But looking at Jimmy's pleading eyes, I said "Well, I'll try."

In the train on our way to Le Havre, I looked again at Jimmy who was stirring, about to wake up. He smiled and said, "I'm hungry Colette, let's go and have lunch."

The restaurant had an elaborate menu. Today, in 1956, food was plentiful, not like in 1947 when I took a train from Marseilles to Paris. Then I was fifteen, excited to be in France, but the war was just over and food was scarce and very simple. Now there was a *prix fixe* menu offering a *pâté de campagne* or a *frisée* salad with walnuts to start, and then a choice of lamb shank cooked in cider, a salmon *soufflé*, a roast beef with truffle potatoes or a *sole meunière*. Dessert was a cheese tray, ice cream or an apple and pear tart. Jimmy chose the *pâté de campagne*, and the lamb shank cooked in cider. I took the *frisée* salad and the *sole meunière*, my favourite fish. Jimmy explained that in New York there was no real sole, only grey sole. I wondered if the grey sole is what we call in France "*Limande*". I told myself that when we were in New York, I would go to the fish market and find out.

I looked at Jimmy savouring his *pâté*. A layer of transparent light brown jelly surrounded it. I stole a bite from his plate. The *pâté* had specks of fat and the herbs, especially thyme, were too overpowering. I was about to say something, but there was a look of such pleasure on his face that I didn't.

The train slowed down and stopped very near the harbour. The port of Le Havre was large and very busy. There were several ships ready to leave and ours at the end of the quay was easily the largest. It was white with blue, red and white stripes painted on its funnel. We slowly walked the length of the quay. This is it, I thought, once we're on the boat there's no turning back.

Going up the plank I looked back at the people milling around. Most of those leaving on the boat seemed young. One teenage French girl on deck was crying. I wanted to go to her and help her, but Jimmy told me we had to follow the porter to our cabin, which was one floor below the main deck. Two beds, a closet, a small bathroom, two armchairs and a porthole through which I could see the sea. The ship rocked gently and already I thought I was going to be sick. I quickly took a pill and hoped that the uneasy feeling I had in the middle of my stomach would soon disappear.

Back on the main deck I looked again for the young girl. I couldn't see her and looked below at the crowd waving their goodbyes. There were no shouts and very little confusion. I thought back to when I left Egypt for France nine years ago. The crowds were shouting, women were crying, and I had felt lonely and sad to leave my Egyptian family for France and an unknown future. Today was very different. I wasn't scared, just sad. Jimmy's arms were around my waist; he was kissing my neck and whispering words to reassure me. The ship slowly glided out of the harbor.

"Let's go to the bar and have a drink to celebrate our new life," Jimmy suggested. As I entered the bar I suddenly knew that I would not make it. I had to be on deck or I would be sick. Back upstairs I found a chaise longue and a young sailor wrapped a blanket around me.

"How do you feel, Miss? Would you like a cup of hot broth?"

"Yes please," I said faintly, thinking I was soon going to be so sick that I would certainly die before reaching New York.

As I drifted to sleep, my thoughts turned to New York. What will it be like living in New York? How would his family greet me, many of whom I had not met? Would I quickly make friends? Jimmy had told me that everyone works in America. Would I also work? And what kind of work could I do? As I dozed off to sleep, I felt better. The boat seemed steadier. Maybe I was wrong. Maybe I would be all right and the crossing would be fine.

An hour later I was awakened by the same young sailor bringing me a cup of very hot *bouillon* and crackers. Jimmy reappeared and insisted that we take a walk around the deck. Later I was back at my chaise until the evening, when once again I tried to go to the dining room. A steaming onion *gratinée* was placed in front of me and I slowly took a mouthful. The warm soup with the golden melted cheese and thick slices of transparent onion tasted great and warmed me. I wasn't feeling too bad and ate the soup with gusto. As we ate, Jimmy talked about his relatives. His favourite was his aunt Edie, his mother's sister. She had never married. She was an executive with Dunhill and she lived, Jimmy explained, with another sister, Gina, also unmarried. Gina kept house for them both.

"Edie is great; she's fun and very intelligent. You will love her and she will love you." Naturally there was also his brother Murray with his wife Naima and their two young children. I knew Murray. In 1948, he had come to my grandmother's house in Paris. In 1949, he had met Naima, his wife, and brought her to our house. But I did not remember her well as they had left for the United States a few months after their wedding.

"My mother lives with them in the summer," Jimmy said, as if he could read my thoughts. I had been afraid that we would have to live with her. Jimmy's mother reminded me of my favourite mystery detective, Miss Marple. I thought she looked like her. Her hair was wavy with curls like tiny sausages at the nape of her neck. She often looked serious and dowdy. I hoped that now we were going to be living in New York, I would get to know her better and we would be friends.

After dinner I wanted to go back to my chaise longue, but Jimmy insisted that I try to sleep in the cabin. As I lay in my bed I tried not to think of the ship's movement. I closed my eyes as I said to Jimmy that I could not stay in the cabin, that I was afraid I would be sick. But I woke up in the morning in bed!

For the next five days life on the ship assumed a routine. I spent a lot of time on my chaise longue, took long promenades, drank hot *bouillon* and only ate once a day. Jimmy talked about the future. He was happy to be going back home. He talked about our living in New York or Boston. He then made drawings of Manhattan, explaining how it was divided in two — East and West — in a grid, and that all the streets had numbers. It was all very confusing. I remembered reading a book by two French journalists about their travels in America. I must have been sixteen when I read it. I was fascinated with the author's tales of New York, the Rocky Mountains, California and ice-cream sundaes.

"I want to try an ice-cream sundae," I told Jimmy, who looked at me with astonishment.

"But why an ice-cream sundae?"

How to explain that the vision of a mountain of ice cream topped with whipped cream, chocolate sauce and a red cherry fascinated me? Could I tell Jimmy that for years America for me was defined by an ice-cream sundae? Never!

On the sixth and last day the sea got rougher and I refused to go down to the cabin. I slept on my chaise wrapped in blankets. The next morning, Jimmy woke me up at five. "Get up! We're about to pass the Statue of Liberty. You must see it."

We stood next to one another. Jimmy was hugging me as we passed this extraordinary statue wrapped in fog. The scene was eerie. It seemed to me that the lady was smiling. She was so tall! Much taller than the one on the Pont de l'Alma, over the Seine in Paris. And suddenly there was New York. I had not expected that incredible vision of a mass of skyscrapers, shimmering in the early sunlight. I was in awe. Viewed from the ship, New York looked beautiful.

As the ship glided slowly down the Hudson led by a red tugboat, I saw that there must have been a major snowstorm in New York; the roofs of the buildings we were passing were covered with snow. I thought of the Paris that I had left just a few days earlier. The parks there were already full of yellow daffodils and tulips under an intense blue sky. So beautiful!

As the ship anchored, I saw people waving on the quay below. I waved back. I recognized Murray and Anne. Jimmy waved too and smiled to me.

"They're down there. Did you see them?"

It was an hour before we could disembark and gather our belongings. Anne embraced me and then Jimmy. She looked sad. Murray stood near her. He was shorter than Jimmy, I thought, with wavy brown hair. And not as handsome. He too looked sad. Jimmy asked what was wrong. Anne blurted out that Edie, Jimmy's aunt, had died a week earlier. They had not wanted him to know for fear of spoiling his last week in Paris. Jimmy cried, he was crushed by the news. I held his hand, trying to comfort him. He blurted out to me "I wanted her to meet you. I wanted her to see who I married . . . Oh Colette, this is so terrible." I felt sorry for Jimmy, but I hadn't known Edie, and with the excitement of arriving in New York, I quickly forgot about her.

The car was waiting for us near a highway. Our luggage baskets would arrive later. On the way to

14

Murray's house no one talked, so I looked out of the window and thought that at street level New York was so dirty and ugly. There was so much snow pushed against the edges of the sidewalks. It looked like a mountain of dirty grey. Where was the beautiful city I had seen from the ship?

We finally arrived at Murray's apartment house on West 77th Street. A doorman in uniform took care of our hand luggage. The apartment house faced a very large brick building surrounded by a garden. "That's the Museum of Natural History," Jimmy said. "A great museum; I'll take you there."

Naima stood waiting at the door of the apartment where she embraced first Jimmy, then me. She was a tall, handsome woman in her mid thirties with jet black hair tied in a bun at the back of her neck. She was wearing a loose dress in bold colours. I would later learn that these dresses were fashionable and made by the Danish designer Marimekko. Next to her stood a cute little boy. "This is Maxwell — he's three. Say Hi to Auntie Colette." Maxwell looked at me and smiled but said nothing. "Later you'll meet John, he's eighteen months and he's sleeping now. Come, I'll show you to your room. We've given you ours, and Murray and I will sleep in the maid's room."

Immediately we protested, but to no avail. I was too young to understand that this would turn out to be a great mistake; taking their room would later provoke fights and create problems. But we were happy to be there and we settled into their room as we were told. For the next few hours, I explored the apartment. It

15

was as large as my grandmother's in Paris, with four bedrooms lining a sombre corridor. The kitchen near the dining room was old-fashioned with a large breakfast table. Later, I joined Naima there as she was preparing lunch. I heard a baby crying. "Why don't you go and pick him up," she said.

As I entered his bedroom, John was standing in his crib. Such a lovely baby! I picked him up and kissed him on his neck. In return I got a gurgling laugh. I knew right away that I was falling in love with him because he looked like Jimmy. I took him back to the kitchen. Naima looked harassed so I asked if I could help. "No, thank you. I have to feed John and Maxwell; you go back to the living room. Another time maybe." I was too shy to insist so I went back to the living room to join Jimmy. Anne was telling him what had happened to Edie.

"She had breast cancer but refused to see a doctor until it was too late."

"What do you mean she refused to see a doctor? Why didn't you drag her there?"

There was silence. I realized that Jimmy was angry, and Anne was upset. I had to do something. How crushing to arrive in a new country and be faced with such horrible news. I was worried about Jimmy. I looked at him, went closer and squeezed his hand with a smile. We shared a glance and I knew we would be fine.

That night, as we sat down to dinner, Naima brought a roast to the table. It was enormous; I had never seen anything like it. Jimmy told me it was a rib roast prepared in our honour.

"Very American," he said with a smile.

A thick slice was placed on my plate with a very large unpeeled potato. "Baked potato," Naima explained, "also very American." I looked at Jimmy to see how I was supposed to eat it.

"Split it in two, add some butter."

The potato was fluffy, hot and tasted like the best mashed potato I had ever had. The skin was crisp, and Naima told me I could eat that too. I discovered that the crunchy skin was even more delicious. The slice of beef was bright pink and tender. I took a bite of the brown crackling fat with a piece of meat. I would have loved to suck on the bone, but no one else seemed to so it was with regret that I left it on my plate.

To this day a rib roast is still my favorite meat, but I always suck the bone clean! Next to the meat was a vegetable I had never seen before. It looked like a small tree and tasted somewhat like cabbage. I thought it was good, but it lacked some garlic or spices. "What is it?" I asked. "Broccoli," Anne explained. "Do you like it?" I didn't really know what to say since I realized that she had prepared it. For my taste, it was too bland. "Strange," I replied, and everyone laughed.

Murray served a very good French wine and told me that in a few years California would produce wines as good as the French. I thought it unlikely, but he was right. Years later, as a food writer, I would go to wine auctions in California and taste wine as good and sometimes better than French wines.

There was no bread on the table and I missed it, especially when Naima brought in the salad. The salad was iceberg lettuce, the same as the American army wives bought at the PX in Germany and served with some strange dressing that they called French. However, Naima's dressing was much better. She was, I thought, a very good cook. I looked around the table at the family. I didn't as yet understand the relationship between Naima, Murray and Anne. There seemed to be tension, but I did not know why. I felt slightly nervous and unsettled, maybe even a bit scared. I looked at Jimmy. He smiled encouragingly and I felt better. Everyone was looking at me, expecting something. But what? Picking up my wine glass, I made a toast to the family and said that the meal was great and that I was so pleased to be there.

The next morning I found my mother-in-law in the kitchen preparing breakfast. Maxwell and John were there too. She was making porridge. She offered me some but I couldn't eat in the mornings and asked for just a cup of coffee and a piece of toast. Jimmy had already left to see some friends and get reacquainted with the city. I didn't really know what to do with myself. I did not want to unpack since I hoped we'd find an apartment of our own before long. I asked Naima if I could help her. She suggested I take John for a walk in the park's playground. Maxwell would be dropped at a playschool. Central Park, I had learned the night before, was the large park near the apartment house. Would I get lost? I was slightly afraid but knew that Naima would explain where the playground was.

While Naima dressed John, I talked to Anne about her plans for the day. "This afternoon, after lunch, I have to visit Gina. She's is very sad and upset," she said.

"Can I come with you?"

"No, some other day, she's not ready to meet you."

I left her and wandered again through the apartment. Murray, who was a financial journalist for the *New York Times*, had already left for work. John was dressed and ready to be taken outside. Naima drew me a plan of the neighbourhood and told me where the playground was. "He can play in the sandbox," she explained. "He also likes the swing. Be careful as you cross streets and don't get lost."

We walked across the street to Central Park. I was astonished. The weather had changed, the sky was blue and the park, as in Paris the week before, showed signs of spring. There were daffodils on the lawns and buds on the trees. I showed them to John, picked up a flower and gave it to him. He tore it apart in two seconds and laughed. He had such a lovely smile but he never said a word, he just laughed.

The playground was surrounded by a cast-iron fence. There were benches all around and in the centre there was a large sandbox with swings on one side and a sort of wooden sculpture on which children could climb. So different from a Parisian park where *Defense de marcher sur la pelouse* (Keep off the grass) is the rule. I plopped John in the sandbox and sat and watched him play. I looked around. Women were sitting talking, and once in a while one got up and said something to her child. I was bored; I should have brought a book with me. A mother, a tall blond woman, came and sat next to me.

"Are you new to the playground? Did you just move here?" she asked.

"Yes."

"Is this your son?"

"Yes."

This was of course a lie. It had flown out of my mouth. Why did I say yes? I felt foolish, but claiming to be John's mother seemed to give me some stature with this woman who started to chat about the weather and the maids in the playground. Pointing to a small girl she said that this one was very nasty. I should watch that she did not hit my son. Suddenly I heard a scream, it came from the little girl. John had taken something from her. I jumped up and ran to him. He had a piece of what looked like bread in his hand. The little girl's babysitter arrived, saying in an angry tone of voice, "Your son took Molly's pretzel. Get him his own," and she pulled the piece of bread away from John. I picked him up and put him back in the carriage. The blond woman walked over again and told me that the pretzel man was at the park's entrance.

"Children love pretzels. You should get him one." Naima had given me a couple of dollars so I bought a pretzel, tore it in two and gave half to John. I bit into the slightly warm pretzel, and spat it out immediately. It was disgusting! Chewy, salty and with a taste of gasoline. I took it away from John, who started to cry, and threw it in the rubbish bin. "Don't cry," I whispered to him, "Colette will buy something good right away."

As I looked at Naima's map I saw that there was a large avenue on the other side of 77th Street, so I walked towards it. I read the sign, Columbus Avenue. Naima had told me that this was where I would find all the shops. I pushed the carriage along the avenue, peering inside the shops. I passed a shoemaker, a butcher, a dress store. The butcher looked nothing like a French butcher. As I looked at the window display I didn't recognize anything, so I continued my walk.

Then I saw a bakery and thought I could get something for John there. As we entered the empty store the woman at the counter asked me what I wanted. I said, "Good morning!" and she look startled. Well, I thought, maybe here you don't greet anyone as you enter a store. In France you have to say "Bonjour messieurs, mesdames . . ." and if you don't no one will serve you. There were long loaves of sliced bread on the shelves, but no baguettes. There were cakes, sweet pastries and, in a bin, round circles of bread, some with sesame seeds. As I pointed to these, the woman said "How many bagels? Plain or with sesame seeds?" So these were the famous treats Jimmy had been talking about in Paris. This was a bagel. They looked good so I asked for a sesame bagel. I gave a piece to John, who stopped crying and sucked on the bread. I took a bite and was very surprised. The bagel was chewy, the crust hard but very tasty, so much better than the pretzel. Happy now, we walked for an hour before heading back to the house.

Back home, Anne was preparing John's lunch. Maxwell would return from school after three, and Naima was out shopping downtown. Once John was asleep in his crib, Anne prepared our lunch and called me in. In front of me was a sandwich. I wasn't sure I knew what it was. White bread, no crust and very soft. The sandwich was stuffed, my mother-in-law told me, with tuna fish salad. It looked a sickening beige color. I took a bite and nearly choked. It was sweet with bits of what I thought was celery. "What's in it?"

"Mayonnaise."

I knew two things: that it was not real mayonnaise and that I couldn't eat it. I looked around, not knowing what to do. When Anne went back to the kitchen I quickly wrapped half the sandwich in the paper napkin she had given me and hid it in my pocket. I told Anne I couldn't eat the remaining half and brought it back to the kitchen. As I sat at the table sipping a cup of weak coffee, I thought of Paris and the ham sandwich in a crispy, baguette I would have eaten in a café. I suddenly missed Paris and felt out of place and lonely. I wished Jimmy was there with me to cheer me up and tell me everything would be all right.

I will never know if Anne realised I had thrown out the tuna fish sandwich, but she never served me another one.

Later that afternoon Jimmy came back announcing that in a few weeks there was going to be a large planner's conference at Harvard. We would go to Cambridge together. Lots of architectural and planning firms would be there, and he could find a good job. I felt better and my spirits rose further when he whisked me away for some sightseeing.

Times Square overwhelmed me. I found it exhilarating with its lights, its immense advertisements, the crowds pushing you around, the traffic. I stood for a while speechless, looking at the large panels of advertising with moving forms. One advertised cigarettes and real smoke was coming out of a woman's mouth. There were so many people, so much noise, and so much colour. I loved it and found it astounding. Then we walked over to Fifth Avenue towards Rockefeller Center. I stood for a while watching people ice-skating in the centre of the complex. Suddenly Jimmy whispered in my ear, "What do you want most from New York?"

"An apartment."

"No, tell me something you want to eat."

"An ice-cream sundae!"

Hand in hand we walked to a small restaurant near an elegant department store called Saks Fifth Avenue. The restaurant, Schrafft's, was on a side street. As we were ushered to our table, I looked around. The customers were mostly women sitting at small wooden tables, eating ice cream or drinking tea. There were banquettes against the walls and the low, round, soft lights gave the restaurant a sort of genteel look. Jimmy ordered a sundae. The dish I had dreamt of for so many years. A bowl of ice cream was placed in front of me. I looked at it in disbelief. It was a monstrous architectural construction. The ice cream was hidden under a mountain of whipped cream with chocolate sauce dripping artistically, topped with toasted almonds. A bright red cherry gloriously crowned it all. It was exactly like the one I had read about years before. But I took one bite and found the ice cream far too sweet and very creamy. The whipped cream was not like Chantilly, the cherry inedible. The dish was so rich that after two teaspoons I couldn't eat any more. I whispered to Jimmy, "Can you finish it?"

Why did I ever think that an ice-cream sundae would be so marvellous? I didn't even like sweets!

We then went by subway to Wall Street. First we stopped in front of City Hall, which looked like a lovely copy of a French chateau. We walked around the park in front of it, and continued on to the Woolworth building. Jimmy explained that the building was famous for its intricate façade.

"I love skyscrapers; there's so much poetry in them. You know, it was the tallest building in the world at the time. Look up Colette. Don't you think it's like a giant towering cathedral?"

I looked up and saw the building with Jimmy's eyes, listening to what he what saying. The building was beautiful! But I did not know if it was as beautiful as a French cathedral and I said so.

"Colette, look at the terracotta skin. It's machine-made and celebrates the world of today; but it's able to produce a version of the medieval stone of Gothic architecture, just like the Gothic churches celebrated, in their own way, the merchants and the artisans."

I wasn't sure I really understood, but I tried to look at New York through his eyes.

Then we walked to Wall Street. The streets in this part of town amazed me; they were so narrow and the buildings were so tall. I felt like an ant crawling in the street looking up and barely seeing the sky. Suddenly what seemed to me an army of people came out of every building, pushing and shoving us.

"What's happening?"

"People are going home, Colette. Downtown is filled with offices and at 5p.m. they all go home. In a few minutes, Wall Street will be deserted. Let's wait and then we can walk around Fulton Street and down to the Battery to look at the Statue of Liberty."

Half an hour later, Wall Street looked like a ghost town, empty and silent. Slowly we walked to the tip of the island and stood together, admiring the Hudson River and the Statue of Liberty in the distance. New York, once again, seemed to me so extraordinarily beautiful.

The next few days went by slowly. I had little to do. I took John for rides in the park, and walked around the neighbourhood for hours. There were no cafés where I could just sit and look at people passing by. I also felt shy about entering a restaurant alone, not knowing what to order. I explored the shops on Broadway, looked at the clothes, the beauty salons. Women, I noticed, had very strange hairdos; their hair was teased and puffed up. I thought as a young woman of twenty-three, I must look very old fashioned with my curls.

Every night, Murray and Jimmy came home late. Jimmy was busy renewing contact with his friends and job hunting. At night he often told me who he saw and what he did. The search for an apartment did not seem to him a priority. We had been in his brother's house for three weeks and I felt the tension in the family building up. There was tension between Murray and Naima — we were still staying in their bedroom — and between Murray and Anne, who spent every summer with them. Dinners were difficult; and there were many silences. Murray would talk about people he had seen without any explanation of why or for what. "I had lunch with the CEO of . . ." or "As the Mayor said to me this morning . . ."

Growing up in Cairo, the conversation was lively and interesting. Here it was more like in my French grandmother's house where no one talked because there was no love between us, or between my brother and I. Here it seemed it was the same. Anne resented Naima, and Naima and Murray did not seem, at least in my eyes, to love one another. I started to dread those dinners. I tried to tell Jimmy about it but he thought I was imagining things.

There was also the problem of the food. Naima was a good cook, but on the nights Anne cooked I ate next to nothing. I was not invited to help in the kitchen and was too shy to offer. I spent these awkward dinners dreaming of a tomato salad, a good Camembert, and above all a French baguette stuffed with ham. I made my escape at lunch. I had discovered a restaurant with no tables, just a counter that felt more like a French café. The luncheonette, Chock full o'Nuts, served a cream cheese sandwich on very good walnut bread. I became addicted to it and went there every day, telling Anne not to wait for me for lunch.

One day I received a phone call from an old friend of my mother, inviting us to dinner. The night of the dinner I went looking for a florist to buy some flowers. I couldn't find any and I was worried. Go to dinner at someone's house and bring nothing? Jimmy kept on telling me it was all right.

My mother's friend was a tall, slim American woman with dyed red hair. Mr and Mrs Lowenstein lived on Park Avenue in a very grand apartment. They had lived in Paris for a year after the war, and this is where they met my mother. "It was a relief to find someone who spoke English so well," Molly said. "She helped me shop and we had a great time together."

Philip, her husband, a banker, was slightly pompous. He made fun of the French, saying they took long hours for lunch and did not work hard. At the same time he told me how delightful my accent was. This was something I would hear time and time again. There were many other guests but I could not distinguish one from the other as everyone was introduced by their first name. I didn't know who was married to whom. The men stood at one end of the large living room and the women at the other. They all drank hard liquor. I was offered whisky but turned it down. I would have loved a glass of wine, but ended up drinking orange juice. The women talked about shopping, babies and babysitters, while I tried to listen to the men's conversation. Their conversation was about politics and the stock market. I would have liked to join them but decided I'd better stay with the women. I had nothing to contribute as I had no children and no home of my own.

Dinner was served from a buffet by a black maid in uniform. We didn't sit at the dinner table but on chairs and couches. I was not used to it, and was afraid I'd spill my food. The whole evening was painful and boring. As we took our leave I thanked Molly for the lovely dinner. "We must see you again soon," she said, as I was thinking that I would have to find friends of my own very soon.

A week later we left for Boston. I was so happy to leave the house and be alone with Jimmy. The city delighted me. I loved the row of town houses around the Green; the scale of the buildings was a relief after Manhattan sky-scrapers and mammoth apartment buildings. On our first night Jimmy took me to his favourite restaurant, a small fish place where we ate broiled flounder and where I had my first taste of clam chowder. The light, creamy broth, filled with chopped clams and cubed potatoes, had a wonderful aroma of the sea and fresh thyme. Oysters followed, thick fatty oysters so different from the French ones, but still wonderful. They slid down my throat in one gulp. The next day we went to Cambridge for the conference on planning. I liked Cambridge with its small streets, its funky boutiques, cafés with students sipping espresso and discussing their classes, books or politics. Jimmy left me for the conference and mingled with his friends while I walked around Harvard Yard. What an extraordinary campus, so beautiful, so free and peaceful! There were students lying on the grass talking or just sunning themselves. I thought of my own experience at the Sorbonne; dreary, immense amphitheatres where the teachers never knew your name. You sat with your friends on hard benches, never meeting the other students. Our only fun was after class, sitting in a café over a ham sandwich and a glass of beer, discussing world politics or Sartre's latest novel.

As I entered the conference hall, there was a woman on the platform talking about American cities and urban planning. I looked at the programme and read that her name was Jane Jacobs, a journalist for *Architectural Forum* and *Fortune magazine*. She was explaining how urban renewal has destroyed American cities by cutting large bands of highway, which was changing neighbourhoods for the worst and killing small businesses. She pointed out how the immense building heights have a dehumanizing effect, their massive blank walls seeming almost hostile to the pedestrians on the sidewalks. I recalled then my own experience of arriving in New York, how I felt like an ant crushed by the heights of the buildings. She added, "We need more people who care. We need to save city centres and stop the exodus to the suburbs." She was passionate and electrifying, and she got a standing ovation. I wanted to meet her but there were too many people. I told Jimmy how much I'd enjoyed the woman's talk.

"We'll meet her in New York, I promise. I know her husband. He's an architect and, like her, fascinating."

That night Jimmy took me to Durgin Park, an immense restaurant packed with tourists like us. There were long wooden tables for communal eating, and we sat next to a family from Ohio with four children. Everyone was very friendly, so different from the French. They were all excited that I was French and questions flew at me:

"How do you like Boston?"

"Love it, it's more like Paris."

"New York?"

"More difficult to know . . . I haven't really explored it yet."

"What part of Paris do you live in? I know the Eiffel Tower and . . ."

It turned out that the father had been a soldier in the war and had visited Paris and enjoyed the visit tremendously. Here the food was different, but also very exciting as Jimmy chose dishes I had never tasted before. A strange corn pudding, light and fluffy, more like a *soufflé* with a very strong taste of corn. I loved it!

"It's called Indian pudding," the woman told me. This was followed by broiled fresh fish and scalloped potatoes. It was the first great meal I had in the United States.

The next morning Jimmy took me to the Italian quarter in North Boston. There was an open market, he told me, like in Paris. All along the street were stands with merchants calling to customers to buy their fare. Oysters piled high, smelling of the sea, clams and large crabs.

"Can we have some now, right here?" I asked one of the sellers who was pushing me to buy oysters. "I don't live here, but I'd like to try them."

"Get yourself a lemon. I'll open some oysters for you. How about clams?"

"I've never eaten clams, I'll try some."

"Bella, anything for your great eyes," he said.

I felt I was back in Italy where we lived after our wedding. There the men compliment you at every corner, bella or not. I bought a lemon and Jimmy and I ate half a dozen oysters and clams. I had never had clams on the half shell. It was a revelation. So different from oysters. You have to chew the clam, and they're soft and hard at the same time, slightly salty, so delicious.

We continued our walk and stopped at a stand filled with vegetables. I recognized Swiss chard and sorrel, but beside them was a vegetable I didn't know. It had broad, waxy, blue-green leaves. Next to it was another vegetable with dark green leaves, frilled with curly edges. "It's kale," the seller told me, handing me a large bunch. I cut a small piece and tasted it. It was spicy and bitter at the same time.

"What are these?" I asked, pointing to the other vegetable.

"The blue-green one is collard greens, and this here lady is mustard green. Buy some and cook it with a piece of salted or smoked pork and you'll love it."

I wanted to buy some but Jimmy said I shouldn't, no one at home would eat it. I promised myself that when I had my own apartment I would try them all. Then I saw stands with lettuces. "I hate iceberg lettuce," I told Jimmy. "I have to bring this lettuce home." I also bought a large, round purple aubergine and some sweet green peppers. The fish stand was great; there were all sorts of fish that were new to me. I would have loved to buy more, but to my disappointment Jimmy said, "We're going back home on the train. You can't take fish with you. It will spoil and smell out the whole compartment."

In the train back to New York I dreaded returning to Murray and Naima's apartment. I began to understand that Murray resented being kicked out of his room and sleeping in the maid's room. We had been staying there too long, and I knew we had to move. On the train, Jimmy told me that he had an interview the next day with a firm of architects and planners who had a great reputation. "I hope I'll get the job," he said. So do I, I thought, so that we can afford an apartment. I also decided that I had to take over the task of apartment hunting. Having made that firm resolution, I felt free to daydream about the vegetables I had just bought and wondered how I would prepare them.

That night I made a sort of *soufflé* with the kale. I thought it was delicious but no one, not even Jimmy, said anything. I put aside my apparent failure as a cook and put all my energies into finding a home. Every morning, the *New York Times* in hand, I walked through the city's streets looking at apartments. Jimmy had been hired as designer and planner at a firm called Mayer and Whittlesey. Meanwhile, the tension in the house was becoming unbearable. Murray had refused to move back into his room. I had the feeling that he and Naima were fighting, and not only about us but also about Anne, who like most mothers-in-law gave her opinion on everything that took place in that house. Dinners were hard to take: Murray barely acknowledged our presence; Naima, wanting peace above all, was busy with the children and refused to intervene. Jimmy was lost in his own world and I desperately tried to make conversation. I talked about the apartments I had seen.

"I saw an apartment on a street called Bleecker. Wonderful! It's on the third floor, a walk up. Great view from the windows and you know, the bathtub is in the kitchen. So romantic! Next to it is a great charcuterie with *prosciutto* and other hams, sausages and cheeses. Also, there are street vendors selling vegetables and fruit. And best of all, the rent is only $85 a month. I want to show it to Jimmy tomorrow. We can move in right away."

My announcement was greeted with exclamations of horror. "Bleecker Street, that's in the village, and a three-storey walk up! The bathtub in the kitchen! Ridiculous Colette, you need a real apartment! Furthermore, it's too expensive."

Too expensive! I heard that statement every night as I would describe what I had found that day. Nothing was good enough for my mother-in-law, nothing was elegant enough for Murray, and Jimmy would smile at me and always say, "Tomorrow you will find something better." I was getting so angry with Jimmy. I tried to explain to him that we were causing strife between husband and wife and that even Maxwell, the three-year-old, was acting up because of it. Jimmy told me I was exaggerating, that things were not that bad and that next day I would find an apartment. Day after day I went looking for a place to live. By now I had learned the bus system and could move up and down Manhattan quite easily. Lunches were a slight problem. I couldn't always find a Chock full o' Nuts and order my favourite sandwich. I tried a street vendor sausage and threw it in the bin; it was nothing like the sausages we used to eat on the streets of Munich. Eventually I discovered the BLT, a tomato and bacon sandwich which I liked, but I had to learn to say "No mayonnaise, and on toasted rye bread." I couldn't eat the thin, soft white bread even toasted.

One night, as Naima was out, I made artichokes stuffed with breadcrumbs and herbs as I had learned in Italy, and cooked them in olive oil. I thought that everyone would be happy, the tension would disappear, and I would be praised as a great cook. But no, no one said anything, not a word. I looked at Jimmy who was wearing his faraway look I now knew so well. It meant that he was thinking of an architectural problem and was totally oblivious to everything around him. Suddenly I decided to leave the house. I'd had enough of this family who did not talk, who seemed not to like one another.

Slowly I got up, left the dining room, put my coat on and waited to see if anyone would notice that I had left the table. I waited ten minutes. Nothing happened, so I left. I walked down Central Park West towards Columbus Circle. By now I knew that part of the city quite well. I sat on a bench outside the park looking at the people walking by. I thought I had made a mistake, coming to New York. I did not like the city, I had no friends, and Jimmy didn't seem to care for me as much as he had in Italy. Everything I did was either criticized or dismissed. What was I doing here? I wondered. I'm twenty-three years old, still young, and I have to go back to Paris, find a job and start a new life again. But I did not want to go back to the apartment. I decided I would stay on my bench until morning and then go back, pack my bags and leave. I must have sat there for over an hour when suddenly I heard Jimmy's voice.

"Oh, I found you! I was so worried; I've been walking for the last two hours. Why did you leave? I was panicky. What's wrong? I don't understand what happened. Please tell me."

I looked at his face; he looked exhausted, upset, there were tears in his eyes. "I love you," he kept on repeating, hugging me. "Why did you do that?" And so I explained and talked about my loneliness, Murray and Naima, Anne and him not understanding, not listening to me. Not helping me find an apartment.

"We've been here over two months. I want my own home with you. I want to find a job. Have a real life." I told him about an apartment I'd found on 68th Street and Central West. "It's set at the back on the second floor. It isn't great, but please could we take it and move?" Jimmy promised that the next morning we would go and see the landlord and sign a lease. We walked slowly back to the house. They had all gone to bed. I did not have to explain anything to anyone.

The next morning, as promised, we went to sign the lease. The apartment had one large living room and a small bedroom which looked out at a brick wall, a small kitchen with a dinette. Jimmy did not seem too happy, but he said nothing. Then we ordered a bed and a few days later we moved in. Murray and Naima were upset with us. We had not asked their advice and they felt offended. Anne thought we should have waited for a better place. No one was happy for us except me.

A few days later my large shipping baskets arrived with my entire trousseau. Together we unpacked and mentally I thanked my mother for the lovely towels and sheets I now had. We went to the Salvation Army and bought two dentist stools for a few dollars and a writing desk that Jimmy stripped and painted white. (Forty years later I still have the writing desk and the stools.) I bought a vase at the Five and Ten and filled it with flowers, because by now I knew where the florist was. I placed one basket in the dinette and covered it with one of the tablecloths I had not wanted to take. This became our dining table, and after buying some pots and pans I was ready to play housewife and cook my first meal.

I was finally home!

Snails with Swiss Chard

Wash 450g/1lb of Swiss chard. Cut the leaves off the stems. Set aside the leaves and chop them finely. Dice the stems. Bring 1 litre/2 pints water to the boil with a pinch of salt. Then add the stems and bring back to the boil. Turn off the heat and drain. In the same saucepan, heat 2 tablespoons of butter, add stems and sauté for 5 minutes or until they are tender, but do not brown.

Then add the leaves and sauté for 4 minutes. Remove from the heat and set aside. Meanwhile in a skillet heat 2 tablespoons of butter. When the butter is hot, add 2 dozen large snails, sprinkle with salt and pepper and sauté for 5 minutes, stirring all the while. Remove from the heat and set aside. Peel 8 garlic cloves. Place the garlic in a saucepan and cover with 225ml/8fl oz of milk. Bring to the boil, lower the heat and simmer for 5 minutes or until the garlic is cooked. Drain the garlic. In a food processor purée the garlic with 120ml/4fl oz of double cream. When ready to serve, add Swiss chard to the snails and heat for 2 minutes, then add cream sauce, mix well and heat through, but do not boil. Serve sprinkled with chopped parsley. Serves 4.

Asparagus with Boiled Eggs

For this recipe you need to choose thick asparagus, not pencil thin ones.

Peel 12 large asparagus and trim ends. Place the asparagus in a large skillet and cover with boiling water. Bring to a boil, lower heat to medium and cook until tender, about 8 minutes. Drain immediately. Place the asparagus, four to each plate, alongside an egg cup. In a saucepan place 4 eggs, cover with boiling water and cook for 4½ minutes (for this dish the eggs should be runny). In a small dish place 4 tablespoons of butter with a few drops of truffle oil (optional). Melt butter in a microwave. Add salt and pepper to taste. Pour the butter into a small milk pitcher, being careful not to pour in the solids from the bottom. Cut off the top of each egg, pour 1 tablespoon of butter into the egg, mix and use the egg as sauce for the asparagus. Serves 4.

Lamb Shanks in Strong Cider

The lamb has to be marinated the night before. In a bowl mix together 2 tablespoons of lemon juice with 4 tablespoons of olive oil, 2 tablespoons of soy sauce, salt and pepper. Place the lamb in a deep bowl, and add the marinade. Turn the lamb shanks several times so that they are covered with the oil mixture. Cover the bowl with foil and refrigerate overnight. Scrape, wash and dice 2 carrots; peel and dice 3 medium size onions; peel, seed and dice 2 tomatoes; peel and chop half a head of garlic. In a large saucepan heat 2 tablespoons of olive oil, add the vegetables, mix well, lower the heat and simmer for a few minutes, stirring all the while. Add 120ml/4fl oz chicken stock 475ml/¾pint strong cider. Bring to the boil, reduce heat and skim the top. Cook for 4 minutes. Remove from the heat, cool and refrigerate overnight. The next day, in an ovenproof saucepan, heat 2 tablespoons of olive oil. Drain lamb shanks and add to the saucepan. Brown on all sides. Remove to a platter and discard the oil. Return lamb shanks to the pan with vegetables and broth. Sprinkle lamb with 1 tablespoon of fresh thyme. Add more broth mixed with strong cider (in equal parts if necessary, as the meat should be covered). Cover with a lid and bake in a preheated oven at 180°C/350°F/gas mark 4 for 2½ hours. Meanwhile peel and quarter 450g/1lb small fresh turnips. Wash 3 celery stalks. Wash and scrape

450g/1lb baby carrots. Cook each vegetable separately in salted boiling water until tender. Do not overcook. Drain and set aside. Remove the shanks from the saucepan. Place the cooked vegetables in a food processor and purée. Pour sauce back into the saucepan, add 2 tablespoons of butter and simmer for 3 minutes, then add the shanks, carrots, turnips, celery and salt and pepper. Heat through. Place the shanks with the sauce and vegetables in a deep serving platter, sprinkle with fresh chopped parsley and serve. Serves 4.

Apple and Pear Tart

First make the dough. In a food processor place 250g/9oz flour with 8 tablespoons of butter cut into small pieces and a pinch of salt. Process until the mixture forms a coarse meal. In a measuring jug mix together 1 egg with 1 tablespoon of oil and 60ml of iced water. Beat with a fork. Then, while the food processor is running slowly, add the oil mixture. It will form a ball. Remove and wrap it in wax paper and chill in the refrigerator for 1 hour. Butter a 24cm/9-inch pie pan. On a floured board roll out the dough. Line the pan with dough and crimp the edges. Peel, core and thinly slice 3 apples. Peel, core and thinly slice 3 large pears. Form concentric circles of apple and pear slices. Dot with 2 tablespoons of butter and sprinkle the top with 2 tablespoons of sugar. Bake in a 190°C/375°F/gas mark 5 oven for 40 minutes. Serve with ice cream or whipped cream. Serves 4 to 6.

Onion Gratinée

Peel 3 large sweet onions and thinly slice. In a deep skillet heat 2 tablespoons of butter, add the onions and sauté over a medium heat until transparent but not brown. Then add 1.8 litres/3 pints of strong beef stock. Simmer for 5 minutes. Correct the seasoning with salt and freshly ground pepper. Toast 8 slices of French baguette. Divide the soup among four ovenproof bowls. Add 2 tablespoons of grated Swiss cheese to each bowl. Top with 2 slices of toast. Place 3 thick slices of Swiss cheese on top of the toasts, dot with butter. Bake in a 190°C/375°F/gas mark 5 oven until the cheese is melted and golden brown. Serve immediately. Serves 4.

Clam Chowder

Wash about 15 very large clams. Place the clams in a very large saucepan and add 225ml/8fl oz of water, 1 medium onion quartered, 1 celery stick cut into small pieces, and 1 bay leaf. Steam covered over a high heat until all the clams are open. When the clams have cooled, remove them from their shells and coarsely chop. Set aside. Strain the cooking liquid and set aside.

In a large saucepan sauté 3 slices of bacon cut into ½ inch-pieces for 4 minutes, then add 1 onion thinly sliced, 1 bay leaf, ½ teaspoon fresh thyme, and 1 tablespoon butter. Sauté until the onions are transparent, then add the reserved clam liquid and 1.3 litres/2½ pints of fish broth. Simmer for 5 minutes, then add 3 potatoes, peeled and cubed. Cook until the potatoes are tender, about 10 minutes. Add salt and pepper to taste. Then add the chopped clams along with 225ml/8fl oz of double cream. Heat through. Serves 4.

Stuffed Artichokes

In a large bowl filled with iced water, squeeze the juice of half a lemon. Using stainless steel scissors cut the tips of four large artichokes. Place them in the bowl with the lemony water while making the stuffing. Mix together 2 tablespoons of finely chopped parsley along with 2 garlic cloves minced, 2 finely minced anchovies, the zest of 1 lemon. Then add 2 tablespoons of fresh breadcrumbs along with 1 tablespoon of olive oil and fresh black pepper. Drain the artichokes. Gently separate the leaves and place about ¼ teaspoon of stuffing in between the leaves. In a large saucepan, heat 2 tablespoons of olive oil. When the oil is hot add the artichokes and brown on all sides. Then stand the artichokes upright. Add 120ml/4fl oz strong chicken broth. Bring to a boil, lower the heat to medium, cover and cook for 40 minutes. Serve at room temperature. Serves 4.

CHAPTER
TWO

Life in New York

We settled into our small empty apartment. We were happy, but I realized very soon that I needed to work. Everyone around me except Naima was working. We also needed the money. In France I would not have worked. At that time young, upper-middle-class women stayed at home, but here in New York it wasn't the same. Until you had children, you were expected to work. When I wrote home that I was looking for work, my mother thought it was odd and replied, "Doesn't Jimmy make enough money to support you?" I was upset by her comments and tried to explain to her that here in New York, there was something in the air that made you want to work, and so I tried to find a job.

Every morning I scanned the newspapers for the "help wanted" ads, but they were all for specific professions or skills, like secretaries or clerks, and I didn't know what I could do or what to look for. My degree in literature was really no help. I spoke English fairly well, but could not spell or type. I had one letter of recommendation from an Italian businessman who ran an import/export company in Udine, Italy, where we had lived. He had hired me hoping I would make a

42

good secretary but then fired me within a week, telling me that I was totally inept. He wanted me to leave without any fuss so he offered to give me a good letter of recommendation. This was the extent of my working experience. I was getting quite desperate and was about to look for a job as a saleslady or babysitter when a small ad for someone who could write in French and in English caught my eye. I called immediately and set up an appointment.

The office of Monsieur Ribaud was on Fifth Avenue near 47th Street, in a building called the Fuller Building. Located at the end of a long corridor, his office was a tiny dark room with two desks, a typewriter and a teletype machine. M. Ribaud was short, slightly bald, his few black hairs held in place with some sort of grease. His shifty eyes were hidden behind thick-rimmed glasses and he wore a shiny grey suit with a shirt whose collar needed ironing. He had a heavy Belgian accent and I tried not to smile when he inquired about my French and my working credentials. With some hesitation I handed him my Italian letter of recommendation. To my relief he barely glanced at the letter, and proceeded to explain that my job would be to read all of New York's newspapers every day. On Fridays I was to write a piece in French, summing up the most interesting articles I had read, and then send it by teletype to Brussels to his newspaper, *La Libre Belgique*. I would be required to be in the office from 9a.m. to 2p.m. every day, and to answer the phone, and for this I would get $35 a week, paid twice a month. I immediately said yes, overjoyed to have a job. I was then handed a key and I promised that I would be on time the next day. I called Jimmy and said excitedly, "I have a real job!"

The next morning Jimmy walked me to the subway, explaining what station to get out at. I looked for my station but I must have missed it, because twenty minutes later I found myself in Queens. I got off the train and tried to ask how to get back to Manhattan. I didn't understand what my would-be rescuers were saying to me:

"You can take the IRT or the BMT to go back to Manhattan."

What did these letters mean? I didn't know what to do and ended up on a bench crying. I was lost, totally lost. As I sat on that bench, forlorn and thinking that I would be fired, an older man approached me and asked if I needed help. As I explained through my tears what had happened, he laughed and told me he would take me back to 42nd Street station. I learned in the subway that his name was Renaldo Butoni, an Italian journalist attached to the UN, and that he lived in Queens. When he left me in front of the Fuller Building he handed me his card and said he hoped we would see one another again, but not on a subway platform. Later, Renaldo and I became quite good friends and he often helped me in my work.

As I reached my office I tried to imagine what excuse I could give M. Ribaud. To my astonishment the office was empty. On my desk were six newspapers, the *New York Times*, the *Wall Street Journal*, the *Daily News*, the *New York Post*, the *Sun* and the *Herald Tribune*, together with instructions on how to teletype the article I would write on Friday morning. The note also said that he would come by on the fifteenth to pay me. M. Ribaud kept his promise, only showing up twice a month, promptly at 9 a.m., staying just long enough to hand me my bi-monthly cheque. I never found out if he or the paper liked my work, or what he did the rest of the time. I was always alone in the office with my newspapers and a pair of scissors.

On the first day I started to read the *New York Times*. I had problems with the political articles since I wasn't familiar with the workings of political parties or the Government, so I turned to local news, which was also quite a mystery to me. Robert Wagner Jr. was then Mayor of New York. There were articles about corruption, others about a mysterious Boss named Carmen DeSapio. Who was this Boss, I wondered? Since I had to wait until the evening to ask Jimmy, I went on to read the next story. This was an article about the controversy surrounding Robert Moses' plans to build more public housing downtown. I doubted that Brussels would be interested, so I turned to the entertainment pages and read about Carnegie Hall and how Mayor Wagner hoped to rescue it from demolition. Musicians and composers all over the country and abroad were gathering forces to protest its imminent destruction. This article was cut out and stacked away. I read about Mayor Wagner's decision to create a free Shakespeare theatre in Central Park. Again I cut out the article and put it away. On Friday I would write an article incorporating all the tidbits I had read.

By 12.30 it was time for lunch and I went to explore Fifth Avenue.

42nd Street was lined with cafeterias and coffee houses. Which one to choose? They all seemed the same to me. I read their menus and wondered what I could eat. What was a Triple Decker? Finally I chose a restaurant that didn't look too intimidating and sat down at a small table. I ordered a hamburger but couldn't remember how to say rare, and I was presented with a grey, overcooked burger, topped with a slice of orange cheese and sweet pickles; it looked and tasted like rubber. I discovered that there was nothing to drink apart from American coffee, which I disliked, and Coca-Cola, which I found sickeningly sweet. I couldn't order a glass of wine or a beer. Unable to eat, I paid and left the place, promising myself that from then on I would bring my own lunch to work.

Back at the office I turned to the *Wall Street Journal*. Scanning the front page I caught a glimpse of American life outside New York. There was a column about a New England woman who had started a business raising Newfoundland dogs and knitting jackets with their hair. The article was fascinating because it was bizarre, and also because the woman was so successful. I cut out the article and added it to my pile. For the next few weeks when I came into the office in the morning, I turned first to the *Wall Street Journal* for its stories on small businesses. They were always fascinating vignettes and, to me, so American. I could combine them with other articles to send to Brussels on Fridays. No one in Brussels ever complained that what

I wrote was often strange or far-fetched. Once in a while I would insert important political news. National elections were to take place the following November so I looked for some extraordinary stories such as the controversy surrounding Adlai Stevenson's shoes. Stevenson was the Democratic candidate for President and the sole of one of his shoes had a hole. An embarrassing photograph was printed on the front page of the *New York Times*. Later I found out that it may have been planted by Stevenson's people.

I enjoyed my work immensely because every day I learned something not only about New York, but also about the rest of the country. Slowly, I began to understand American politics and the workings of New York City.

New York life fascinated me, and especially Greenwich Village. Very often, after work, I would take the subway, get off at 8th Street station and walk through the Village. It was late June, and along the narrow curving streets the lovely town houses had geraniums in window boxes and flowers everywhere. I spent my afternoons looking at the small funky boutiques, sat in coffee houses or spent hours at the Sheridan Square book store. On weekends, Jimmy and I would go to listen to jazz or see an avant-garde play. We often went to the first in-the-round theatre in New York, the Circle in the Square Theater. I can still remember how enthralled I was to see Jason Robards in *The Iceman Cometh*, or Truman Capote's *The Grass Harp*. The crowd was young like us, and after the play or concert we would walk to 10th Street to the Ninth

Circle for a drink or dinner, or stop on Cornelia Street for a cappuccino at Caffe Cino. It seemed to me that people all around me were adventurous, that they were open to new ideas and very involved. I felt that there was hope, excitement in the air and found the city vibrant and alive. For me the Village was a bit like the Left Bank in Paris; it felt like home.

Every morning I looked forward to going to work. I was no longer afraid of losing myself in the subway. The only problem I had to solve was my lunch. Every day after work I went shopping for food in our neighbourhood. I found supermarket displays baffling, and the food was always wrapped in plastic. If I wanted to buy beef or lamb, the cuts of meat were different from those in France, and it took many attempts before I knew which one to buy. Bread was also a problem until I found a delicatessen which sold rye bread, far tastier than the sliced, white supermarket bread. I also discovered that New Yorkers liked smoked salmon, and that it was as good as what we used to buy in charcuteries in Paris. I also loved Virginia ham, very different from my beloved French boiled ham; it was slightly too sweet for my taste, but with it I could still make a very good sandwich. Finding good vegetables and salads was also a problem. String beans seemed to me overgrown, nothing like the French *haricots verts* I was used to, and I hated iceberg lettuce. At first we went out to dinner, but very soon this became too expensive so I started to cook.

One night we decided to invite Jimmy's old friend, Gabriel Sedlis, an architect from Europe who had come to the United States after the war. He had been Jimmy's classmate at Harvard. I can still remember this first dinner because I had to comb the neighbourhood to find what I wanted. I made a cucumber salad with plain yogurt, garlic and mint. Fresh mint was then not easily available in local supermarkets. I finally found a small store run by an Italian woman who had fresh herbs growing on her window sill. She agreed to let me have some. I also bought some chuck steak to make my own hamburgers and served them with a green peppercorn sauce; I made a purée with tinned artichoke hearts using my new blender, a present from my mother-in-law. The purée was good if too thin and slightly watery since I had overdone the blending. But no one complained. For dessert I made my first apple mousse, a great success, because I had just discovered how wonderful Mackintosh apples are.

My reputation as a good but somewhat bizarre cook began with this dinner. As time passed I became more adventurous and went beyond my Westside neighbourhood to shop.

One day Jimmy announced that he had invited another old friend from Harvard for lunch the following Saturday. "Don't make anything too French or too strange," he said, "I haven't seen him in several years and I don't really know what he's like." Not too French? I decided to make an *omelette*, a salad and a cake for dessert. I had been attracted by boxes of luscious cake mixes and learned that you could make a cake by just adding water and baking it in the oven. And so I started with the cake. When the cake came out of the oven it looked nothing like the picture on the box. I had not understood the instructions and had ended up baking the chocolate icing, and using the cake mix as the icing. That cake ended up in the bin. As I prepared the *omelette*, I remembered Jimmy's request. I decided that, in order not to make it too French, I would add some ketchup to give it an authentic American touch. The friend was charming, but the lunch was an unforgettable disaster. When I brought the "American" *omelette* to the table, Jimmy looked astonished as he stared at the disgusting greyish-orange mass. Not knowing what to do I immediately started to talk about my total lack of cooking experience, hoping that Jimmy's friend would forgive the horrible meal. The friend smiled as he played with his food. Jimmy looked grim and as I was getting more and more nervous, I endlessly chattered away. As he was about to leave, he looked at me and said he hoped I would enjoy discovering New York's restaurants. We never saw that friend again and Jimmy made me promise to never attempt to make what I thought were American dishes.

During the week we ate simply, shopping only at our local supermarket, but on weekends we explored downtown and the Lower East Side. Our first stop was often the Essex Street market. The market was alive and bustling with people. The meat stands were run by Italian butchers. There I was able to find fresh chickens, rabbits, lamb and cuts of beef or veal I could recognize. The vegetable stands offered at least three types of salad greens, and I could satisfy my desires for a tender lettuce (which I learned very quickly was called Boston lettuce, reaffirming my strong belief that Boston knew good food) or *escarole*. There were bright red tomatoes, fresh string beans (maybe not as thin as the French ones, but still quite good), large Italian aubergines, bitter sorrel and broccoli. I often bought broccoli to try to prepare this uninspiring vegetable in a more imaginative way. With it I made soufflé, tried it in soup with turnips or served it steamed, drizzled with olive oil bought in Little Italy. It took me much longer to be adventurous enough to buy fish because I could not recognize any except grey sole.

I also explored Jewish stores on Houston Street. There I found fresh bread, fresh or baked farmer's cheese, thick cream and dried fruit. What I liked best was the butter. On the counter was a mountain of bright yellow butter, just like in France. The butter was sweet and creamy, so much better then the packaged variety sold in my supermarket. The saleslady would cut the butter with a wire to exactly the amount I needed. Then we would stop at Gus' pickle store on Essex Street and Grand and buy a quart of sour cucumber pickles. They were so crunchy and so garlicky that I could not resist the temptation and ate most of them on the way home. Nearby was a store that sold bagels and bialys. Jimmy had introduced me to my first bialy. I loved the hot, fresh, chewy bread with its chopped onion centre. I would buy dozens and have them for breakfast slathered with butter.

Then we would walk to Katz delicatessen for lunch. The restaurant was like nothing I had ever experienced.

At lunchtime it was packed with people who, I was told, came from all over the city to eat pastrami sandwiches, which I disliked, or steamed corned beef, sausages or brisket, which I loved. Along the wall was a small army of men carving the meats. I adored the thick, fatty sandwiches of steamed beef brisket. My favourite moment was standing at the counter, mouth watering, famished, watching the old man carve the brisket with such dexterity and rapid movements that I was totally mesmerized. Smiling, he would always offer me a thin slice of hot, fatty brisket for my approval. I would say "Great! Delicious!" and my sandwich would be so thick and moist that the bread would invariably fall apart. It was so succulent that I picked up the pieces with my fingers. Full and satisfied we would make our way to Bleecker Street.

On Saturdays, Bleecker Street was lined with carts piled high with salads, two or three types of aubergines, leeks or green peppers. Along the street we stopped at Italian stores offering salamis, hams, cheeses, fresh Parmesan and what I liked most — sweet Italian sausages that I would serve the next day for lunch with sautéd green peppers. There were several bakeries with crisp Italian baguettes that were not as good as the French bread I was used to, but certainly a great improvement on the supermarket bread. Back at our apartment, I would cook dinner with the things I had bought: I would make a potato and leek soup, stuffed chicken with garlic, and steamed fresh spinach. On weekends I liked to bake those large Idaho potatoes — I was then in love with this quintessential American way of preparing a potato — but to be different I would often top them with herb butter or fresh ricotta from Bleecker Street.

In the evening we would stroll along Broadway and often go to the Thalia, a small avant-garde movie house that showed foreign films.

My tranquil routine at work lasted only a few months. An international crisis was looming, and suddenly everything changed. The United Nations was in full session to examine the Middle East crisis after Egypt and its leader Nasser nationalized the Suez Canal. The French and the English attacked Egypt; the Soviet Union sided with Egypt, and the Security Council called an emergency meeting of the General Assembly to discuss the problem. I was quite worried as I still had some family members living in Cairo. M. Ribaud reappeared in my life, arriving in the office in his rumpled suit, saying that from now on and for the duration I was to attend UN General Assembly and Security Council meetings and write daily reports for *La Libre Belgique*. He himself would write the weekly article to send home.

I called on Renaldo, my Italian journalist friend, to help me through the labyrinth of the UN, and every day for several weeks I sat and listened to the arguments from both sides. At lunchtime Renaldo and I would stroll to a small Italian restaurant not far from the UN where I would nearly always order a plate of *spaghetti bolognese* or veal *scaloppini* with clams and a glass of red wine. Sleepily I would go back to the General Assembly meetings and doze off my lunch while listening to the Israeli-French arguments and the Soviet Union response. Often the sessions would last late into the night and I would not come home until the wee hours of the morning. Jimmy did not like coming home to a dark house and no dinner. We argued a lot about this new development, but I was so excited and interested that in the end he accepted the situation. Then, when the UN sessions ended, I went back to my old routine of reading my daily newspapers.

M. Ribaud reappeared a few weeks later to announce that a Belgian State Senator was arriving in New York. The Senator needed a translator to accompany him to Washington, where he had important business to discuss with members of American Government. M. Ribaud offered me the job and said that I would be paid $100 a day, for three days — a lot of money for us — plus my usual salary of $35 a week. This was my first trip to Washington and I was told that the Senator would put me up in a nice hotel. Worried about me being alone with the Senator, Jimmy let me go only reluctantly, making me promise that I would call every day.

Senator S. was a tall, portly man, dressed in a grey pinstriped suit and shiny black shoes, with a red handkerchief in his breast pocket. He looked more like an actor playing the role of a Senator than a real one, but I was quite impressed. During the train ride to Washington he explained that I was to help him secure an appointment with the newly appointed Secretary of State, Christian Herter. Senator S. knew how to reach him; the American Consul in Brussels, who was his friend, he added, had given him several telephone numbers. We registered in the hotel and as Senator S. had no address in New York, he suggested that we use mine. I started to make enquiries and quickly discovered that you could not get an appointment so easily, even if you were a Senator from a friendly but small country like Belgium. I was told to call again the next day so I convinced the Senator to take me on a tour of Washington. The city delighted me with its wide avenues and its great monuments that felt so much like Paris.

That night Senator S. left me alone to dine at the hotel while he went to visit some friends. Shy and lonely, I ate in my room and spoke to Jimmy for hours knowing that the Senator would pay the bill. The next day I tried and again failed to set up an appointment. I was about to give up when a message came that the next day the Senator could meet with the then Under Secretary of State, Robert Murphy. Murphy would decide if a meeting with the Secretary of State was warranted.

From our hotel we walked to the State Department and were greeted by Mr Murphy. When we had sat down I heard for the first time the reason for our trip, as I was asked by Senator S. to translate. Senator S. stated that he represented Belgium's right-wing political party. They were very concerned with the results of the future presidential elections. They had raised a million dollars and he was empowered to offer the money to Eisenhower's campaign for a second term. I looked up at Mr Murphy and thought that he was going to explode. He jumped up, red in the face, and told us to get out of his office and never, never appear before him again. Shaking and scared, I translated what Mr Murphy had said: It was totally illegal for a foreign country to interfere in American politics. S. wanted to argue, but I insisted that we leave straight away. I realized that we had made a fatal mistake. Back at the hotel I told Senator S. that I would go back to New York immediately, as he no longer needed my services. Could I be paid? He promised to send me a cheque and said he would take care of the hotel bill. Relieved, I left for New York.

I took the next few days off and went back to work on the following Monday. When I arrived at the office, I was astonished to find it totally empty. The desks and the teletype machine were gone. The superintendent of the building told me M. Ribaud had moved out, and when I called the only telephone number he had given me, I discovered it was disconnected. I called the newspaper in Brussels and was told that he had been fired three weeks earlier. He had never told me, and had left the country without paying me! I checked every day for mail, hoping to get a cheque from Senator S. But nothing came. I called his hotel in Washington but was told he had checked out. I called his hotel in New York but was told they had not heard from him. I was angry and upset; I felt both men had used me. A few days later, as I was preparing dinner, the bell rang. I opened the door and was confronted by two men in black suits looking stern and very official. They asked if they could come in so I called Jimmy to the door.

"It's the FBI. They want to talk to you. We have to let them in."

Suddenly I was afraid.

"The FBI? What is the FBI? Some sort of police?"

"Never mind Colette, I'll explain later. Just answer their questions."

They began by asking me dozens of questions. When did I meet Senator S.? And M. Ribaud? Did I know that he had signed the hotel bills in Washington and New York and had given my telephone number and address as the person in charge of paying the bills? No, I did not know. I tried to explain that I had just met him, that my job was to accompany him to Washington and translate for him. I was even more frightened when I learned that he had bought an expensive fur coat in Washington with a phoney cheque, that he had gambled in underground betting places and had lost huge amounts of money, and that he had given my name and address as the person in charge of his office. I was devastated, and petrified. As they left, the two men implied that I could be deported and sent back to France.

That night neither Jimmy nor I could sleep.

"Jimmy, what if they deport me? What a disaster! And I didn't even get my three hundred dollars. If they deport me, will you come with me? Do you love me?"

I cried on his shoulder while he tried to comfort me.

"Of course I love you. I didn't know I had a criminal for a wife — much more exciting. Stop crying. The truth will come out. You were innocent. This is America, nothing can happen to you." Then he added,

"I'm starving! Let's eat. Let's go to the kitchen and have some French scrambled eggs." Drying my tears I made scrambled eggs and went to bed feeling a bit less scared.

For the next couple of days we heard nothing and no one came to our door. But on the third day the two agents reappeared. It turned out that the Belgian Ambassador in Washington had cleared me. I learned that M. Ribaud and Senator S. were both criminals and not members of any political party. The FBI apologized for scaring me and left.

Years later when I ran for political office as a council woman for my neighbourhood I found out that the FBI had a dossier on me, and that for a few years they had monitored my career and activities.

I was unemployed once more and began to search for another job. In early September I spotted an ad for a French teacher at the Convent of the Sacred Heart on Fifth Avenue. When I was growing up in Cairo my mother, who came from a Jewish family, had converted to Catholicism. When I was seven, she had decided that I should also be a Catholic and registered me as a boarder at the Convent of the Sacred Heart in Cairo. I stayed at the convent until I was fourteen. When I saw the notice, I felt that as an alumna I had a good chance of landing the job.

The Convent occupied a magnificent old house on Fifth Avenue and 91st Street. In my youth there were two orders of nuns: the Mothers, who were upper class and well educated and wore elaborate habits, and the Sisters in simpler garb who cleaned the school and cooked. Now, two decades later, the order had changed. The Mothers' habits were different and simpler and there were no longer any Sisters. I was interviewed by the Mother Superior and tried to play up my background as an alumna of the Convent, and despite my obvious lack of experience was given the job. The salary was $3500 a year which seemed a fortune to me after my $35 a week. I would teach the seventh, eighth and tenth grades. Instructed to appear at 8.30 a.m., I would attend the general meeting and morning prayers, then teach my classes. Lunch was served at 12.30, and classes would resume at 2 p.m. I had several free periods where I could sit at my desk in the teacher's room and prepare for my classes. I was handed a weekly plan book and was told that the Mother in charge of studies would look at my book from time to time. "One more thing," the Mother Superior added, "we have a very important marching band which competes in Cardinal Spellman's marching band competition, and this year we want to win. If you have students in your classes that belong to the team, their practice takes precedence over French lessons." (As far as I know during my tenure at the Convent they never won.) And so my career as a French teacher began.

I quickly discovered that I loved teaching and was good at it, but I had problems with the Mother in charge of studies. She would pop into my classes just as I was telling a story about Paris or writing a funny rhyme on the blackboard. She thought my plan book was far too disorderly. She also thought that I told too many stories in class (which I did), that my method of teaching lacked discipline, and worst of all that I did not follow the curriculum. I did attempt to change the way I taught and to follow her directives, but soon I became bored with the planned lessons. To my mind making the learning of language fun was more important than her strict teaching rules. I continued to tell stories about growing up in Paris, sang songs and played games. Often I had nothing to do because most of my students were part of the marching band, and rehearsals took them away. The students were for the most part children of wealthy Catholic New Yorkers. I learned from the other lay teachers that the majority of students would end up next door at the Duchesne School, the Convent's finishing school, and not go on to college. Those who did go to college usually went to Marymount, a Catholic university. At my first parent-teachers meeting I was relieved to discover that my students loved their French classes, and that the parents were very pleased with my performance. At Christmas I was showered with gifts. There were bottles of French perfume, scarves, leather gloves, but most of all, box after box, of expensive writing paper from Tiffany ("You must write home to France often", explained one of my students, giving me yet another box of writing paper), so that for the next two years I had a sizeable credit at the store, though never quite enough to buy myself a nice Tiffany bauble.

Anne, who lived alone during the winter in Coral Gables, Florida, asked us to join her for the holidays. Jimmy, who for a while had gone to school in the

South, wanted to show me Florida and see old friends. Christmas had always been very important to me. At boarding school in Cairo I would wait impatiently for the Christmas holidays, hoping to see my mother, who I seldom saw, and spend some days with my grandparents whom I loved. Most Christmases, my mother would forget that I had holidays; she would be travelling somewhere, but my grandmother, knowing how disappointed I would be, showered me with gifts. Waking up in the morning I would run into our large salon, and there in a corner would be a pile of presents: books; games; dresses; lovely gold bangles; sweaters, and many other things.

I wanted to make our first Christmas in New York special. We decided to spend Christmas Eve together in our house, then the next day we would fly to Florida to visit Anne. I bought a small Christmas tree, decorated it only with lights, and placed presents all around it. Our relationship with Murray and Naima had cooled but on weekends I often took John and Maxwell to the park, so when they asked us to join them for Christmas dinner we accepted. I offered to cook the dinner as Naima had cooked for Thanksgiving. This started a tradition that lasted for ten years. Naima and I took turns in preparing Thanksgiving and Christmas dinners. A genteel, unspoken rivalry began: Who was the better cook? Who had the most imagination?

For that first Christmas I became obsessed with the dinner. I wanted to make everything special. I spent hours talking to Jimmy about it and devised an elaborate menu. I would make a five-meat *pâté* to start, followed by a goose stuffed with chestnuts and apples. I would also stuff the goose's neck with the goose liver and Italian sausages as I remember my French grandmother doing it, and prepare a carrot soufflé and sautéd potatoes with rosemary and pine nuts. Dessert was more of a problem since I was not a very good pastry cook. I thought that caramel poached pears would be the easiest.

To find all the ingredients we needed, Jimmy and I spent the weekend before Christmas roaming the Village and the Lower East Side. We bought dried chestnuts and Italian sausages in Little Italy; for the *pâté* I bought chicken breast, chopped pork, veal and fat back in a small pork store I had found on Ninth Avenue. The goose was a problem. When I asked the local butcher he answered that he had never sold a goose before. He told me that a turkey was what normal people made for Christmas, or perhaps a ham? But I *am* a normal person, I thought, and I want to make goose! I was about to give up on the idea when walking down Bleecker Street I saw a butcher's with a sign in its window that read "Wild Game". I went in and asked about goose. "Of course I can get you a goose," said Mr Ottomanelli, who owned this wonderful store with his brothers. "However," he added, "I'm not sure I can get a fresh one; it might have to be frozen."

On the following Thursday I proudly returned home loaded with a frozen goose, some chicken livers and fresh herbs. This was to be my first attempt at cooking a goose. I had found kosher salt which was quite similar to the coarse sea salt my grandmother used and, mixing it with minced garlic, I rubbed the goose inside and out with it and refrigerated it until Christmas.

On Christmas day I removed all the salt, slid large pieces of butter under the skin of the breast, rubbed the goose with more butter and, hoping for a golden goose, put it in the oven to bake for four hours. It had been decided that I would prepare the rest of the dinner at my sister-in-law's house. Jimmy was to bring along the goose later, closer to dinnertime. I had instructed him to baste the goose from time to time and add some broth to the pan if he saw that the liquid was drying up. I then walked over to my sister-in-law's house with the other ingredients. At around seven o'clock I received a frantic phonecall from Jimmy. He had forgotten the goose and had never basted it. It had been in the oven for more than five hours, the pan looked black and please could I rush over. The goose was cooked!

I thought I could save it and told him not to tell anyone what had happened. I carved as much meat as I could, arranged it on a platter, and then proceeded to make a creamy sauce with lots of butter, double cream and some of the drippings from the roasting pan. I covered the meat with the sauce, sprinkled it with chopped parsley and brought it back to the house. The *pâté* was a success, so was the *soufflé* and the potatoes. No one commented on the goose except to say that it was quite an original recipe. Years later when I told Naima what had happened, she laughed and said, "And we all thought you had served a very special dish from France! No one dared say it wasn't very good."

The next day Jimmy and I flew to Miami. In 1956 Coral Gables was a large community of mostly retired couples. Anne's house, like most houses there, was built in the Spanish style with a red-tile roof, blue-green shutters, and ochre-stuccoed walls reminiscent of the Mediterranean. She had a lovely garden and I was delighted to find that she had fruit trees loaded with bright, large lemons, grapefruit and limes, and a jungle of banana trees. What pleased me even more was to find behind the house a mango tree like the one we had in Cairo. I hadn't tasted a fresh mango since I'd left Cairo ten years earlier. The sweet-smelling fruit brought back memories of trips to the mango market with my Egyptian grandfather. In Cairo's market there were many types of mangoes: some flat and round, some small and bright yellow, or very fat in deep purple, red and green. Here in Florida, the red mangoes were enormous and very juicy. I sat in the garden and ate my first American mango with relish.

That night Jimmy insisted we go to a barbecue rib restaurant on Tamiami Trail called Shorty's. "Barbecue ribs are the best thing in Florida", Jimmy explained. "You have to try them and you'll find out that we have dishes here as good as anything you will find in France." The restaurant was unpretentious. The room was barn-like with wooden tables and benches, and everyone sat together. In the back was an open pit where ribs were slowly baked over hickory-wood coals all day and all night long. We ordered several racks of ribs. The ribs were covered with a reddish-brown sauce, a mixture of tomatoes, onions, herbs and hot spices, and when they were placed in front of me, an unexpected aroma of a winter fire, of wood burning wafted towards me, promising slightly scorched but succulent meat. Grabbing a rib I tore the meat off the bone, sauce dripping down my chin, and laughed with pleasure: the meat was tender and juicy, the best pork I had ever tasted. With the ribs we ate steamed corn, on the cob, another dish I had not had for a long time. In Cairo the ears of corn were slowly roasted on coals. They were tough, slightly burnt; here the corn was young, tender, dripping with butter, and very sweet. With the meal we drank large pints of ice-cold beer and very soon, slightly drunk, we were talking with every one around us at the table. They asked the usual questions once they found out we didn't live in Miami. Where do you come from? Up North? No, I'm French, and as in Boston I was immediately asked how I liked Miami. I don't know yet, I haven't seen anything, but I'm sure I will love it. The ribs are so good!

For the next few days we swam in the ocean and drove through Miami Beach in the evenings. The hotels astonished me; they looked like bad copies of Versailles, or large Renaissance castles with added towers and plaster sculptures everywhere. They were aqua, pink and blue, and everything was so big, so vulgar and so exaggerated that it left me baffled. I just wanted to go back to Anne's lovely garden with the mango tree and to the incredible sandy beaches at Coral Gables.

During our stay in Florida, Jimmy and I would have to endure a number of exasperating social occasions. One morning Anne announced that her friends at the club were all inviting me to lunch, alone. Alone? A lunch just with women? I had never heard of such a thing!

"Jimmy, I don't want to go. Lunch with just women! Horrible." But Jimmy said I had to go, if only to please his mother. And so I went.

The country club resembled Cairo's country club, with manicured lawns, a club house, a swimming pool surrounded by deck chairs and umbrellas. But what was very different was the golf course which spread far beyond the club house and was spotted with electric golf carts silently zooming around. The luncheon event was held in a private dining room overlooking the eighteenth hole. The room was full of women with white hair tinted blue, most of whom were wearing pink or light-blue trouser suits. I was introduced to Ethel who immediately handed me a box filled with a lovely white orchid. Holding the box in one hand I did the rounds: Ethel, Sally, Molly, Rachel, Helen, names and more names swirling around me. I no longer knew who was Sally and which one was Helen, but kept on hearing whispers behind my back:

"So young, so very French, what a lovely accent, like Hildegarde! Anne must be so very happy."

Finally we found our name cards — I was placed between Anne and Ethel — and we all sat down. It was then that I made my first mistake. I opened my orchid box, removed the orchid, and plopped it in my glass of water to cries of astonishment and horror from my host who was sitting next to me. "This is a corsage. You must pin the orchid to your dress," she said, "don't put it in water!" I apologized, removed the dripping orchid and pinned it to my dress just above my breast. Very soon my dress around my breast was soaking wet and I looked ridiculous. I unpinned it, placed it next to my plate and smiled, and since all the women were looking at me I attacked the first course: large, chilled, boiled shrimps surrounded by a familiar, pink, slightly sweet cocktail sauce.

I tried to talk about New York, my experiences at work, but no one was really listening. They were more interested in local gossip: which widow was flirting with whom and who was giving a party for New Year's, what to wear, etc. Anne whispered that Ethel was giving a very lavish New Year's party, and that we were invited but not everyone at the table.

The next course came along and Ethel, to everyone's approval, announced loudly that she had ordered it in my honour: Chicken *Cordon Bleu*. I looked down at my plate. Lying there was a piece of chicken breast wrapped in what looked to me to be ham and covered in a beige, slightly gelatinous sauce. As I took a bite, all eyes were on me. To my mother-in-law's dismay I said in a very loud voice, "It is quite good but it is not French." There was utter silence, and I realized then that I had made another major mistake. Trying to save the moment Anne changed the subject, saying that I had spent most of my childhood in Egypt and probably did not know French cuisine all that well. From their looks I knew that Anne had now made a mistake too. I was no longer this lovely French girl but some strange Egyptian creature. I could see in their faces what they were thinking: "Poor Anne, look what she got. A strange foreigner, an Egyptian at that . . . she must be so upset." I tried to save the situation as the dessert, a rich chocolate cake, was placed in front of me, and I exclaimed in the most French accent I could muster that this was the best cake I had ever had. But the damage was done. Nobody cared!

New Year's Eve was yet another trial. I dressed very carefully and told Jimmy I was afraid of the luncheon guests who would be there, but he just laughed and said all of them would have forgotten about me. Anne added that it was a privilege to be invited, as not all of her friends had been.

"You're going to have a lovely time. The food there is always delicious." I thought of my lunch and sighed in despair. Jimmy laughed at my sad face and said, "Come on, Colette. It won't be so bad! Cheer up, we're all going together. It'll be fun."

The house was immense, in pink stucco with red Spanish roof tiles, arches and a lovely patio with a fountain in the centre. Women wore long flowing dresses and men wore suits in iridescent dark blue or white jackets. Again I was introduced as Anne's new French daughter-in-law. Very soon I was surrounded by several men all talking at the same time. I heard them whisper, "You know Frenchmen are lazy — they take two hours for lunch. Also, when you visit Paris and they spot you as a foreigner, they raise their prices. You can't bargain with them. After all, they forgot that we liberated them." Someone added: "All Frenchmen are drunks, they drink wine all the time . . . even for breakfast!" This avalanche of criticism astonished me. I was about to respond when one man, slightly drunk, added that he was eagerly waiting for midnight so that he could kiss me. "What a treat! A real French girl!" and everyone agreed that it would be a great thing to do. At that point, upset and on the verge of tears, I went to look for Jimmy.

"Take me home. I hate it here. Please take me home . . ."

And so we left. Back at the house we lit a fire and Jimmy tried to comfort me. As midnight approached Jimmy kissed me and whispered: "Happy New Year in your new country. Let's make love in front of the fire, and let's make a baby!"

The next morning I knew something in me had changed: my breasts felt rounder. I felt full and very happy, sure that I was expecting a child. Anne had been quite upset by our early departure the night before, but Jimmy explained that everything was so new for me that I had felt homesick for Paris. She accepted his explanation and forgave me.

A few weeks later I discovered that I was indeed pregnant. We decided we needed a larger apartment and found one in a building in the Upper West Side, not far from Naima and Murray's house. It had two bedrooms, a small dinette, a large living room and windows that overlooked the street. We bought some furniture: a couch, two chairs and a dinette set. The large wicker baskets were put away, and we were ready to invite our new friends for dinner.

We invited Gabriel Sedlis and his girlfriend, Peter Greenquist, a young man who had gone to Europe with Jimmy in 1949 and was working in a publishing house, and Michael Brill and his wife, Judy. Michael, an architect like Jimmy, was funny and very fat. He loved food and it was amusing to cook for him. That night I went all out. I prepared a *choucroute garnie*, a French sauerkraut dish cooked in Champagne with sausages, smoked ham and boiled potatoes served with French mustard. With it I served hot Italian baguette and fennel salad. The guests oohed and aahed and said they had never tasted such delicious sauerkraut. I had found the sauerkraut in the Lower East Side, the sausages uptown in the eighties in a German neighbourhood and the fennel in Little Italy. We drank lots of wine, talked about politics, the state of architecture, the future, and what a great cook I was. I was proud and happy.

As I was going to bed, I thought, "This is my life, this is my home. I am going to have a baby." For the first time in many years, I felt I belonged somewhere. I was sure that the whole world was open to me, that in New York nothing was impossible and that I could do anything I wanted.

Cucumber Salad with Mint

Oriental cucumber is long and narrow and has fewer seeds than the regular cucumber. Peel and thinly slice 2 oriental cucumbers. Place the cucumbers in a bowl. In another bowl beat together 350g/12oz of plain yogurt; add ½ teaspoon lemon juice and 1 tablespoon olive oil,

1 garlic clove minced, and salt and pepper to taste. Mix well and pour over the cucumbers. Then chop 2 tablespoons fresh mint leaves. Add to the salad and mix well, then refrigerate until ready to serve. Serves 4.

Hamburgers with Green Pepper Sauce

Shape 675g/1½ pounds of ground beef into 4 hamburgers. In a large skillet heat 1 tablespoon butter with 1 tablespoon olive oil. When the oil is hot add the hamburgers and cook to desired doneness. Remove from the skillet and keep warm. Meanwhile add 1 tablespoon butter to the same skillet and scrape the sides. Add 1 small onion thinly sliced and sauté until the onions are transparent, then add 225ml/8fl oz chicken broth, salt and pepper and 1 tablespoon of green peppercorns. (These are available in jars in any gourmet store or supermarket.) Simmer for 5 minutes. Place the hamburgers on a platter, pour the sauce over them and serve. Serves 4.

Artichoke Purée

Drain 2 × 225g/8oz tins of artichoke hearts. In a skillet heat 1 tablespoon olive oil. When the oil is hot add the hearts and sauté for 3 minutes. Then remove from the heat and cool. In a food processor place the artichokes, 2 eggs, salt and pepper, 2 garlic cloves, 1 tablespoon thyme, 1 tablespoon flour and 60ml/2fl oz double cream. Process until all the ingredients are puréed. Return the purée to a saucepan and cook for 5 minutes stirring all the while, adding 1 tablespoon fresh butter at the last minute. Serve sprinkled with chopped parsley. Serves 4.

Chicken with Garlic

This recipe is for 1.6kg/3½ lb chicken. Wipe the chicken and place in a large bowl. In a small bowl mix together 1 tablespoon lemon juice with 2½ tablespoons olive oil, 2 tablespoons mushroom soy, salt and pepper. Pour the mixture over the chicken and refrigerate for 2 hours. Meanwhile peel a whole head of garlic. Remove the chicken from the refrigerator. Slide some garlic cloves under the skin of the breast; place a handful of cloves in the cavity. Place the chicken in a roasting pan with the sauce from the marinade. Surround the chicken with the remaining garlic cloves. Add 225ml/8fl oz of water to the pan and roast in a preheated 180°C/350°F/gas mark 4 oven for 1 hour, basting the chicken from time to time. Remove the chicken from the oven. Carve it and place on a serving platter surrounded by the garlic cloves. Add 225ml/8fl oz of chicken bouillon to the pan, heat, correct the seasoning adding salt and pepper to taste and add 1 tablespoon fresh tarragon. Pour the sauce over the chicken and serve with roast potatoes. Serves 4.

Goose with Chestnuts and Apples

Today one can find already peeled chestnuts which I find much easier than cooking and peeling them yourself. Goose is often available frozen. If you can, try to find a butcher who will get you a fresh goose.

Wipe and remove as much fat as possible from a 4.5kg/10lb goose. Keep the fat for the neck. Cut off the neck, setting aside the skin. Rub the goose with 150g/5oz coarse salt and refrigerate overnight uncovered. This will help dry the skin and allow the fat to escape more freely during cooking. The next day wipe away the salt. Peel 4 garlic cloves and slice. Make incisions in the goose's skin and insert the garlic. Rub the goose with soy sauce, and sprinkle it with 3 tablespoons of dried tarragon and freshly ground pepper. Prick the goose's skin all over. Place the bird on a rack in a large roasting pan. Add 450ml/¾pint of chicken bouillon to the roasting pan. Preheat oven to 190°C/375°F/gas mark 5. Roast the goose for 15 minutes at that temperature. Then reduce the heat to 170°C/325°C/gas mark 3 and cook for 4 hours. From time to time remove the fat from the roasting pan. (Keep the fat in a jar to be used during the year for cooking vegetables or meats.) The goose is cooked when the leg moves easily. Remove the goose from the oven and allow the bird to rest for 15 minutes before carving. Degrease the juices in the roasting pan. Add 225g/8fl oz of chicken bouillon, salt and pepper, tarragon and simmer for 5 minutes. Serve the sauce on the side. Serves 6.

Goose Neck Pâté

Remove all the fat from the skin of the neck. With a needle and thread sew the neck to form a pocket, leaving only an opening large enough for a tablespoon. Chop the reserved fat into small cubes. Cube the goose liver as well as 3 chicken livers. Mix the fat, the goose and chicken livers and 225g/8oz of Italian sweet sausage meat. Add 1 egg and 1 tablespoon flour, salt and pepper, 2 garlic cloves minced and 1 tablespoon cooking brandy. Mix well. Spoon the liver/sausage into the neck, pushing it down as you fill it. When the neck is full, close the opening with needle and thread. Place the goose neck alongside the goose and cook for 3 hours. Remove from the roasting pan, cool and refrigerate, wrapped in foil overnight. The next day, thinly slice the goose neck and serve with crackers and a salad as an appetizer. Serves 4 to 6.

Poached Pears with Caramel

Peel 4 pears. In a deep saucepan place the pears side by side. Add 675ml/1¼ pints of water with 150g/5oz of sugar and 85g/3oz of raspberry jam. Bring to a boil, lower the heat and cook for 15 minutes or until the pears are tender when pierced with a fork. Remove the pears to a serving bowl. Cook the liquid until reduced to 225ml/8fl oz. Pour the juice over the pears and refrigerate. Just before serving make the caramel. In a heavy bottomed saucepan place 280g/10oz of sugar with 2 tablespoons water and ½ tablespoon lemon juice. Melt the sugar over a low heat, stirring all the while until the melted sugar turns a golden brown. Pour the caramel over the cold pears. Garnish with fresh mint and serve as is or with whipped cream or vanilla ice cream. Serves 4.

Choucroute Cooked in Champagne

Wash under cold running water 1.8kg/4lb of sauerkraut. In a large saucepan cook over a medium heat 150g/5oz of cubed, double-smoked bacon until well done. Add the sauerkraut, mix well. Then add 10 juniper seeds, 10 peppercorns, and ½ bottle of Champagne. Mix well, lower the heat and simmer for 1 hour, stirring from time to time. Then add a 450g/1lb piece of smoked bacon, 1 kielbasa cut into 3-inch pieces, 4 smoked pork chops and simmer for another hour. Add more Champagne if necessary. Five minutes before the dish is ready boil 4 German frankfurters. Serve the Choucroute with boiled potatoes, plenty of French bread and good Dijon mustard. Serves 4.

CHAPTER
THREE

Exploring New York: Chinatown, Little Italy, Brooklyn, Atlantic Avenue

Marianne was born on 27 September 1957, a cool autumn morning. I took a leave of absence from the Convent to take care of her. After barely two months, I received a frantic call. My replacement was a disaster. The students hated her and parents were complaining. Could I come back sooner? I was breast-feeding Marianne, enjoying being a mother, and the prospect of teaching again so soon did not appeal to me. But we needed the money and when the Mother Superior said that my schedule would be changed to allow me to go back at noon to feed the baby, I accepted. But then I was faced with a big problem: I needed a nanny. All the ones I interviewed were very expensive, and we had very little money at the time. I put an ad in the local paper and Frau Zeimnitz came into our lives.

A Viennese woman living in the United States for over thirty years, Frau Zeimnitz had been a governess for wealthy Upper East Side families. She was married but had no children, and I never did meet Herr Zeimnitz. Now retired, she was bored and missed looking after children. The Fräulein was a short, bosomy woman, and looked something like an oversized keg of beer. She was in her late sixties and wore a drab grey suit that matched her hair. I was slightly frightened of her and wondered if I really should let her take care of my baby. But I had no choice. "I can pay $35 a week," I explained, "and you have to be here promptly at 9 a.m. and stay till 3.30 p.m." This was, even at that time, a miniscule salary. I was sure she was going to refuse, and I then would have an excuse not to go back to work. Instead she answered in an imperious voice:

"Show me the baby!"

We went into Marianne's room to look at the tiny sleeping baby. Marianne opened her eyes, smiled, and went back to her dreaming. Fräulein scowled, looked around and barked:

"Where is the carriage? And where are her clothes?"

And I knew then that Fräulein was here to stay. I showed her Marianne's dainty knitted dresses that my mother had so lovingly made; the sheets with embroidered blue jumping rabbits and pink dancing elephants, both of which I had never used. I explained that my mother, who lived in Paris, had copied Princess Grace of Monaco's child's trousseau, hoping that her first grandchild would be as well dressed. With a cluck of her tongue, Fräulein approved.

My Uncle Clément had sent me an enormous classic English carriage, which I disliked because it was, for my taste, too ostentatious. Upon seeing the imposing, deep-blue lacquered carriage with its matching blue canopy embroidered with Marianne's initials, Fräulein's tongue clucked furiously, like a hen that had just laid the perfect egg. I realized that I had nothing to fear and could go back to work without worrying about my daughter.

A year went by without incident, and I was rather naively unaware of what was going on around me. My life gravitated around Jimmy, my child, and my teaching. I was getting used to New York, we had new friends, and my English was quickly improving. On weekends Jimmy and I would take Marianne for walks in Central Park or explore other parts of the city. We would stroll down Mulberry Street, through the heart of Little Italy. Mulberry Street was lined with Italian restaurants. We would stop for an Italian espresso and a piece of *torrone* at Ferrara's on Grand Street. Sometimes we'd shop at Di Paolo, a grocery store packed with salamis, hams, mozzarella and cans of imported tomatoes. I would try out my Italian with the owner's son while he thinly sliced some *prosciutto* or compared the different *pecorino* cheeses that were displayed on the counter. As we walked home, laden with Italian goodies, I tried to imagine what I was going to cook that night: maybe spaghetti with fresh tomatoes and mozzarella or veal chops covered with a layer of *pecorino*.

Although I was teaching my salary was not high enough to complement what Jimmy was earning. We were always broke. I wondered what else I could do. I placed an ad offering my services as a translator in the *New York Times*. I received many calls and got an assignment to translate business documents for a bank. The documents were technical and boring, but the job helped me write better English. I worked late at night when Marianne was asleep and Jimmy was working late in the office. It was during that period that Jimmy's office called to say that he had had an accident and was in the emergency room at the New York Eye and Ear Hospital. Someone had thrown an eraser which hit his eye and tore his cornea.

When I got to the hospital I was sent to the intensive care unit. I waited for the doctors to let me in, and when I was finally able to see Jimmy I was horrified: both his eyes were bandaged. Was he blind? A young Chinese doctor was standing next to him. As I bent down to kiss him and hold his hand, he whispered to me, "Colette, I am so scared. These eyes are my life. What will happen if I can't see? What will I do?" I turned to the doctor.

"I am Dr Chen, Suzanne Chen," she said. "He will be fine. His cornea was torn, but not badly. He will heal, but it may take weeks. We will keep him here, and I will look after him. Please don't worry and tell him not to worry. I promise, he will see, but he has to rest and keep his eyes closed. We have to prevent his eyes from moving so the wounded one heals faster."

I looked at Jimmy again. He looked sad lying there with his head on the pillow, his eyes covered by two heavy bandages. She repeated several times as she turned to leave:

"Don't worry, he'll be fine. I'll see him later."

"You'll be all right. I liked her, she would not lie. Please don't worry. I'll be here with you. I'll read to you and stay next to you. It's only a week until you come home."

That afternoon I stayed with Jimmy, and then went home to reorganize my life. Now I would need a baby-sitter every day after Frau Zeimnitz went home. I would have to organize my classes so I could run to the hospital and see him at lunch and then again at dinner. The nuns were very kind and allowed me to switch my classes so I could be free at noon. Frau Zeimnitz agreed to stay until after dinner so that I could spend some time with Jimmy.

Dr Chen came to see Jimmy several times a day and chatted with him. She was a beautiful young woman, thin and petite with straight, dark black hair and a wonderful warm smile. Together they talked about China and her family. I thought it strange that she spent so much time with Jimmy. Was I jealous? Maybe, but I resolved to befriend her.

I learned that Dr Chen was born in Shanghai, but at the age of two had escaped with her parents to Hong Kong, fleeing the Japanese invasion. When she was twelve, as China was becoming communist, she had been sent to New York to her mother's family and had gone to school here. She became interested in becoming a doctor at a very young age. Her parents came much later with her two brothers, one of whom was an architect who worked for a firm that Jimmy knew. Doctor and patient talked about architecture, politics and food.

Food at the hospital, as expected, was horrendous, so every day I cooked something to bring for Jimmy's lunch then returned home and cooked his dinner. But what do you cook for someone who is bored, lying in bed, his eyes closed, having nothing to do but listen to music and eat? The food had to smell good and taste even better. This was quite a challenge. I bought a hot plate so I could reheat some of the dishes I brought along. I roasted a chicken and served it at room temperature with a cold tomato sauce; another day, I served it with a spinach and tarragon sauce. I made a sweetbread salad with raw mushrooms and julienne fennel, and I poached salmon and served a green mayonnaise to go with it. I grilled sliced aubergine served with a lemon vinaigrette and made his favourite, a meatloaf with pork, veal and beef that he could eat cold the next day.

At every meal, Jimmy insisted we play a game. I was to describe what was on the plate, the colour, the texture of the food I was about to serve him and how it was arranged. Then he would describe the taste as he bit into a piece of chicken or fish. It was through playing this game that I learned to talk about food in vivid language and describe a dish so well that, as Jimmy told me later, he could see it.

Ten days later Jimmy was discharged with one eye still bandaged. Dr Chen proposed coming to the house regularly to see how he was doing. Jimmy was quite pleased with this arrangement. I, on the contrary, thought: Is all this personal attention usual? I didn't know, but I decided that it would be best to please Jimmy. I invited her for dinner the following week. Over dinner, we talked about food, culture, and Chinese customs. It was a wonderful evening, and suddenly I didn't mind that she took such an interest in Jimmy. From then on, she came at least once a week to check on his eye and have dinner. She always arrived with some new ingredients: a sauce, a Chinese vegetable or some strange sweets for Marianne. She would talk about architecture and Chinese politics with Jimmy, about her family and food with me.

One Sunday I received a phone call from Suzanne inviting me to go shopping with her in Chinatown. I jumped at the opportunity. Jimmy and I used to go shopping in Chinatown, but beyond buying fresh fish and fruit, we did not venture very far. To go with Suzanne would be a great adventure. And so one Sunday morning in February, Suzanne and I walked down to Chinatown.

Chinatown then was not as spread out as it is today. It was a small triangle of streets bordered by Canal Street, the Bowery, and Worth Street. Its main shopping streets were Mulberry and Mott. The restaurants were around there too, but also on the little crooked streets:

Elisabeth, Pell and Baxter. The streets were teaming with people buying food for the holidays since Chinese New Year was only a few days away. As we passed some restaurants delicious aromas invaded the street. I was famished, although it was only ten o'clock.

Looking at me, Suzanne could tell I wanted to eat something and suggested we have a bite before starting on our shopping adventure.

"Follow me; I know a small *dim sum* place on Baxter Street. The *dim sum* is Cantonese and really fresh."

I had had *dim sum* with Jimmy before, but we always went to a restaurant full of other "Genjis" (foreigners), never to an all-Chinese place. This restaurant, located on Baxter Street, was jammed with people, eating and wildly chatting. Young Chinese women pushed steaming carts from table to table, chanting the foods they hawked. Suzanne knew the owner, so we immediately got two seats at a big round table with eight others. She stopped the first cart and chose three different steamed dumplings, then from another cart chose what looked like a large white noodle stuffed with shrimps. As the third cart approached I saw chicken feet.

"Can we have some of these?"

"You like chicken feet? Americans never eat them."

"But I'm French. When I was a child, my grandmother made soup with chicken feet. We would eat them with coarse salt. I loved them."

First Suzanne taught me how to use chopsticks, and served me my first dumpling. The dumpling skin was very thin, translucent, and was stuffed with bits of shrimp and pork. They were served with a light soy sauce with julienned ginger. Delicious! Then came small round, steamed dumplings.

"Pick them up with your spoon, and be careful they are full of broth."

The dumpling squirted spicy hot broth into my mouth, and were filled with chopped pork, bits of mushroom and ginger. Simply luscious! I could have eaten a dozen. The third dumpling was vegetarian, filled with minced spinach, chopped scallions and peanuts. Fantastic! Next I tried the wide noodles stuffed with shrimps. They were like a very white, thin *crêpe* filled with shrimps and steamed, and were served with a light soy sauce. Its bland taste was in complete contrast to the crunchy, spicy ginger-coated shrimps.

Then I attacked the chicken feet. They were totally different from my grandmother's boiled chicken feet. These tender, golden-brown feet were cooked in a sweet soy sauce. They were soft on the outside with crunchy centers. I was in heaven; I'd never tasted anything so wonderful. We then had lightly fried Hakka-style stuffed tofu. Suzanne explained that each Chinese province had a different cooking tradition. Hakka food, which she had loved ever since her stay in Hong Kong, came from the north of China. Their cuisine, she said, was a mixture of sea and land. Fish, seafood, pork and chicken. The simple triangles of tofu were stuffed with dried shrimps and cubed peppers, then lightly fried. They were very different from the steamed dumplings we had just tasted — less spicy, but far richer.

Later, as we walked towards Mulberry Street, Suzanne said we were going to Mott Street to pick up a live fish.

"At New Year you must always buy live fish, and steam it with its head and tail. The fish brings good luck to the family."

The fish store had a giant tank near the window filled with a variety of fish I had never seen before. Large black ones with whiskers, small fish that looked like dorade, silver fish, and many more. Suzanne asked for a large fighting fish. The man serving us picked up a net and looked at the fish in the tank. He pointed at a large black fish that was swimming swiftly. Suzanne agreed and the man placed the fish in a large plastic bag. The fish was really fighting, hitting his tail against the bag. We both laughed — this was a true fighting fish.

We then walked down the street to a large grocery store that sold vegetables, meat and poultry.

Outside the store were trays filled with several Chinese mushrooms. Some of them had cracked caps showing white streaks. These, Suzanne told me, were more expensive than those with the normal brown caps. The cheaper kind were for soups and the expensive ones were used in main courses with Chinese broccoli or with sautéd chicken. The expensive ones would very soon become my favourite as I learned how to soak them for several hours to make a delicious mushroom *consommé*. Suzanne then pointed to some dried yellow sticks which she explained were bean curd that could, after being soaked in water for an hour, be tied into knots and added to stews. From that day on my *boeuf bourgignon* would never again be the same.

We bought cellophane noodles and three sorts of soy sauce; the mushroom dark soy would also become a staple in my kitchen as I used it for marinating quails or fish. We also picked up dried snow fungus, which looks like a dried white Chrysanthemum (they don't taste like much, Suzanne said, but added to any dish the fungus will absorb the flavour of whatever is cooking), lily buds, wood ears and cloud ear mushrooms. Then we looked at the fresh vegetables. Suzanne suggested that I first try the dark-green, long string beans.

"Try them with sautéd Chinese chives; they will taste very much like your own French haricot beans."

I also bought some flowering Chinese broccoli. As she chose the vegetables, Suzanne would cry out their names:

"This is cilantro, like coriander, and stronger than parsley."

"This sausage-like vegetable is fresh lotus root."

"This beautiful twisted thing is fresh ginger root."

"This big potato is in fact taro root. The Chinese use them in stews, make a purée or deep fry them."

As we walked along the poultry aisle she pointed to a black-skinned chicken.

"My mother makes a broth with them whenever we have the flu. She says it makes you strong. These tiny brown eggs are from quail."

I told Suzanne that from now on I would come every week and shop in Chinatown. She laughed and said I would need her to translate, since very few people in

Chinatown spoke English. And so a tradition evolved where once a month I would meet Suzanne to shop. Jimmy would meet us later and we would dine in one of her favourite restaurants. I learned that the restaurants that catered to Chinese had two different menus: one for the Chinese in Chinese, and one in English. I also learned that the strips of coloured paper on the walls with Chinese writing were the specials of the day. Once we went alone to a restaurant that Suzanne had often taken us to, and I asked the waiter for one of the dishes on the wall. He shook his head and said emphatically "No," but I insisted and so he brought me a dish that looked awful. Giant worms swimming in a heavy sauce was what it resembled, and it tasted like rubber tires. I had ordered sea slugs! From then on, whenever we went out with Suzanne and her family, I took down the names of the dishes I liked and Suzanne would write them in Chinese so that I would be able to spot them on the walls.

Slowly my cooking changed. I became bolder in using Chinese ingredients in French or American dishes. I served Chinese mushroom *consommé*, rubbed a roast chicken with dark soy sauce, made a French purée with taro root and served steamed spinach with sautéd lily buds. My friends would always ask before taking a bite, "Colette, what's that floating in my soup?" Or "I like those crunchy vegetables, what are they?" I gained the reputation of being a weird but excellent cook. I also started to read about China and its culture. My dream was to visit China and experience for myself the dishes that Suzanne used to talk about, but said were not available here.

On warm, sunny days Jimmy and I would walk across the Brooklyn Bridge into Brooklyn Heights, where we had friends. With them we would parade down the promenade overlooking the East River, and sit in the sun admiring the vista of skyscrapers of Lower Manhattan. I liked Brooklyn Heights with its narrow streets and lovely town houses; it reminded me more of Europe than my Upper West Side neighbourhood. It was on one of our walks in Brooklyn that I discovered Atlantic Avenue and its Middle Eastern food stores. The discovery would change my life.

After leaving Egypt in 1947 for Paris, I had consciously shunned my Egyptian past, desperately wanting to be French. I had worked hard to lose my singsong Egyptian accent, learned to dress as I imagined a French young woman would, and never looked back at my Egyptian past. Now being French in the United States seemed to be my passport to a better life; in New York, everything French had cachet. As Jimmy and I walked past a store on Atlantic Avenue, I stopped short as I noticed a cascade of loofas hanging on a nail. Loofas! These were the vegetable sponges that Aishe, my maid, washed me with when I was a six-year-old girl until my skin was as red as a lobster!

As I stepped into the shop — the Oriental Pastry and Grocery — the smell of cumin and coriander hit me with such force that I staggered. I was back in Cairo in the kitchen with Ahmet, sitting on the counter, eating a pita filled with warm, lemony *ful medamas* (richly braised fava beans). A smooth male voice said, "*Ahlan wa sahlan*". Without thinking, I repeated the familiar greeting. The words came out without my knowing that I could still speak some Arabic.

I looked around at the shelves filled with food I remembered: jars of *tehina* and *tarama*, buckets of briny vine leaves, jars of rose petal jam, honey, and tiny stuffed aubergines. On the floor were barrels filled to their brims with multiple varieties of rice, small red and black lentils, dried brown beans from Egypt, and a panoply of macerating olives — pickled, cracked, oiled, peppered. There were also pickled onions and lemons that I remembered using in stews, and my favourite: bright pink turnips pickled in beet juice and vinegar to eat with *ful*. Near the counter were baskets of fresh pita breads which I had not seen in more than ten years, and in a corner, in a jar, were paper-thin sheets of apricot paste that we used to roll around ice cubes and suck like lollipops in the summertime. I wanted to buy everything.

The voice I had heard belonged to a man with curly black hair and a warm smile who stood behind the counter. How did he know I would understand? And did I? I thought I did, but I wasn't sure. Shy and afraid of making a mistake, I responded in English, "Why me?" "*Habibi*," (my dear one), "you look Egyptian or Lebanese," he said laughing. I asked for a jar of *tchina*, a pound of *ful medamas*; and wondered if he had *mulukhiyya* (a bitter green herb used to make a popular soup in Egypt). "Yes, of course . . . two kinds. You want dried or frozen?" I didn't know, but having an aversion to frozen foods, I chose dried and was handed a large bag of brittle leaves. I asked for cumin and coriander, two loofas, a pound of olives and a container of pickled turnips. Then with a loud, happy *Ma' al-salaama* (good-bye), laden with my purchases, we set off for home. On the way, I promised Jimmy that he would have a great dinner that night.

Back home, as I looked at all the food, I suddenly realized that I had no idea how to prepare any of it. In Cairo, no girl in my family was allowed in the kitchen. The kitchen was the cook's domain. True, I had managed to sneak in without my grandmother noticing. Ahmet, our cook, who liked me, would plop me on the kitchen counter and let me taste whatever he was preparing. I looked, smelled, ate, but nothing more. *Tehina*, I remembered, was a light creamy sauce, not that thick oily paste I had in front of me. What should I do with this enormous bag of *mulukhiyya*? The soup I loved was a smooth, deep-green soup, redolent of garlic and cumin, and was served with a mound of steamed rice. How did one transform these dry leaves into that lovely soup? *Ful medamas* was served with pickles and slices of hard-boiled egg. But what had made the whites so brown? I didn't know, but I thought that I could cook the beans and do without the eggs. I boiled the beans for two hours, tasted them; their skins were too tough, they were nothing like the warm, soft ones Ahmet would give me to taste in a fresh pita bread. That night we ended up eating pickles, olives, bread and cheese. I promised myself that the following weekend I would go back and ask the owner of the store how to prepare the dishes I longed for.

The following weekend, I dragged Jimmy back to Atlantic Avenue. Mohammed, the owner, upon seeing me again so soon, affectionately called me *sukkara* (honey, sugar) and was willing to explain everything to me. Pen and paper in hand, I took notes. He told me how to make a good *tehina*, with water and lemon juice; that dried *mulukhiyya* had to be pressed through a very fine sieve and added to strong chicken broth along with cumin, coriander and garlic. He explained that *tarama* was mixed with soft white bread and lemon juice, and that *ful* had to be soaked overnight and slowly cooked for nearly twenty-four hours. "It is much better to buy cans of *ful*. All you have to do is heat them and mix them hot with lemon juice, olive oil, salt and pepper."

Atlantic Avenue was like a slice of Cairo to me with all its Arab shops. There was, for example, a larger, more elegant store across the street from Oriental Pastry called Sahadi, selling foods from all over the Middle East; further down the street were two bakeries (more Syrian than Egyptian), a butcher and one or two Yemenite restaurants. I was eager to return home to try once more to cook an Egyptian dinner. The *tarama* turned out perfectly, creamy clouds of lemony caviar-flavoured mousse, just as I remembered. I tried to squeeze the dry *mulukhiyya* leaves through a fine sieve, but my fingertips were scraped and I decided that next time I would buy the frozen version. Miraculously, the soup turned bright green and its garlicky, grassy aroma summoned Jimmy to the kitchen. I had succeeded. The food was good, but not quite what I remembered. Jimmy loved it. Soon I started to cook Egyptian dishes for our guests.

Later I went further, remembering my grandmother and Ahmet's other dishes, and tried from memory to reproduce exactly what Ahmet had cooked in Cairo. I made stuffed vine leaves and cooked rice the Egyptian way; I made *sambvsaks*, small pastries filled with cheese, and baked chicken on a bed of leeks. To my surprise, I had, through memory, become an expert cook of Egyptian dishes.

Something else also changed. Gradually, I began to recall with a certain pleasure small incidents from my life growing up in Cairo. I would tell Jimmy about my grandmother's poker day and how Tante Marie would give me some money if she won; or about my grandfather who took me to Cairo's mango market. I even sang Arabic songs to Marianne. From then on, I often spoke about my life in Cairo to friends. I was no longer ashamed of my past, and to everyone who asked where I came from, I now answered, "I'm half French, half Egyptian," to the chagrin of Eunice Whittlesey, the wife of one of the partner's in Jimmy's office. She would state in an authoritative voice, "You don't look Egyptian . . . you look French." I had a problem dealing with people like Eunice who thought of me as too loud, too Mediterranean and probably just a bit too sexy. Jimmy tried to explain their reaction as naturally Waspish, more reserved, but that didn't make me feel any better. I preferred to spend time with Americans of

92

European background, and happily, most of our new friends were just that.

Another chance encounter introduced me to an entirely new way of understanding the art of cooking. I met the Japanese artist Arakawa and his wife, the American poet, Madeline Gins. Arakawa loved good food and believed that my cooking, which mixed Asian and French ingredients, was fantastic. He thought I should also get to know Japanese cuisine. He talked about dishes I had never heard of, like *soba*, buckwheat noodles that you eat cold, or *shabu shabu*, a dish of thin slices of meat that you twirl in a hot broth. I made him a French *potée*, a dish of poached meats and vegetables served with an *aïoli* sauce; and while you eat you also sip the rich, golden broth. The dish resonated with Arakawa as it had the same basic idea as his beloved Japanese dish. He loved it, and promised then and there to introduce us to a real Japanese dinner.

One night he invited us to a Japanese restaurant on 57th Street, at the corner of Park Avenue. I don't remember its name, but I will never forget the meal.

I had walked along Central Park on my way to meet them at the restaurant; I had a feeling of wellbeing. It was an early autumn evening; the sky was clear and a crisp breeze rustled the red and gold leaves. I felt alive and happy. As I arrived at the restaurant I was ushered to a beautiful private room whose floor was covered with tatami mats. We sat on the floor on silk pillows around a lacquered table. In a corner was a tall black vase holding one apple tree branch with tiny pink flowers. The first course was a soup served in miniature teapots. The teapot lid held a little cup and in the cup was a thin slice of lime. I was told by my host to squeeze the lime into the soup, drink the broth and then eat the morsels from the little teapot. The broth was clear and warm, with a faint taste of fish and flavoured with a mushroom that I learned later was the famous Japanese *matsutake* mushroom. The zest of the lime came from a citron called *yuzu*, whose perfume made me swoon. In a single moment I was warmed by the delicate broth, enthralled by the tastes and texture of what I discovered in my little teapot: a shrimp, two Gingko nuts and several bits of mushroom.

Absorbed in the ritual of the dish I realized suddenly that this extraordinary soup echoed and prolonged the feeling of calm energy inspired by my autumn walk to the restaurant. The remaining dishes were as extraordinary an experience as the first one: a golden broiled fish, sweet and spicy, swimming in a transparent broth topped with shaved white radish and seaweed, tingling like the autumn breeze. *Sake* was served in delicate china cups, and at the end of the meal we were brought warm smoky tea. For dessert, grapes peeled and threaded onto a beautiful, carved wooden skewer, with overlapping slices of bright orange persimmon.

I fell in love with Japanese cuisine. Like a visionary dream, the experience of this meal opened up a new world to me. I quickly realized that this was how I wanted to cook. I knew then that I hoped to create a cuisine that would stir emotions in my guests, respond to seasons, and tighten bonds between friends sharing this experience. I realized the importance of the actual container in which the food would be served. I roamed the city looking for beautiful, unusual porcelain from China, Japan, France, Italy or the best American pieces. I searched New York for Japanese ingredients (they were difficult to find, but Arakawa helped), for French and American miniature vegetables, for Chinese mushrooms, spices and fresh fish. I strove to bring elements of surprise and mystery to the table. I decorated my table with branches from our garden and I garnished dishes with fresh flowers. My friends, astonished by my dinners, begged to be invited and so once a week, Jimmy and I gathered our friends and our children together for a meal where most of the recipes came out of my imagination.

As the new autumn semester started, I found out a year after Marianne was born that I was pregnant again. Jimmy felt ambivalent about having another child; he thought it was too soon. But I was elated. When I announced to my mother-in-law that the new baby would be born in May she was very upset, and within a few weeks sent us a television. I guessed, with an inner smirk, that she thought the television would distract us from more amorous activities. I told the Convent that I was expecting a baby in May, and the Mother Superior's reaction took me by surprise. I was called to her office. Her face was set in a grim expression and her mouth was pinched into a straight line. I wondered if one of the student's parents had complained about my teaching.

"Sit down. Mother Elisabeth told me you are expecting another child," she snapped.

"Yes, at the end of May. But don't worry . . . I have someone who will replace me for two months. She is excellent," I assured her.

"We cannot renew your contract," she countered, her bonnet shaking furiously. "You are a good teacher, but we believe that mothers should take care of their children," she continued in a more compassionate tone. "Your child needs you, so we've decided that this will be your last year with us. We hope that when your daughter is old enough to go to school you will consider the Convent. We could make some financial arrangement."

"But this is not fair!" I objected, forgetting the intractable nature of the Mother Superior. "Marianne is fine. I have an excellent babysitter." I was crushed. Didn't the Church teach that marriage centred around procreation? How could they do this to me? Here I was pregnant again and losing a job that I loved.

"But the Church says . . ." I attempted.

"Don't bring the Church teaching to me!" Mother Superior roared. "The role of a mother is to stay with her children. You *must* give these children you teach a good example. Now, go back to your class." It was obvious to me that she wouldn't budge.

What were we going to do? We needed the money and I wasn't sure I could get another job so easily. Back home that night I tearfully told Jimmy what had happened. Jimmy told me not to worry, that another job would come along soon. He was now making more money since he had become one of the senior designers in his office and we could live on his salary alone. He patted my arm, kissed me and said, "When do we eat?"

Chinese Mushroom Consommé

This is a very simple recipe made with dry shiitake mushrooms.

Remove the stems of 8 large Chinese dried shiitake mushrooms. Place mushrooms in a bowl and cover with 1.4 litres/2½ pints of hot water. Soak for 2 hours. Remove the mushrooms and thinly slice. Place the mushrooms in a saucepan along with the mushroom water and 120ml/4fl oz chicken bouillon. Add salt and pepper to taste. Bring to a boil, lower the heat and simmer for 10 minutes. Pour the soup with mushrooms into six bowls, add 1 small spinach leaf to each bowl and serve. Serves 6.

Fennel Soup with Coriander

Thinly slice 3 fresh bulbs of fennel. In a large saucepan heat 1 tablespoon butter. Add 1 onion thinly sliced and sauté until transparent. Then add 3 litres/5 pints of chicken stock. Add the fennel and 2 large potatoes, peeled and cubed. Bring to a boil, lower the heat and cook until the potatoes are done. Purée the soup. Pour the soup back into the saucepan, add salt and pepper to taste, heat through. Pour the soup into 6 individual bowls. Add 1 tablespoon of crème fraîche to each bowl and sprinkle with 1 tablespoon chopped coriander. Serves 4 to 6.

Mushroom Flan

Clean and remove the stems of 675g/1½ lb of crimini or portobello mushrooms. Purée the mushrooms in a blender with 4 large eggs, salt and pepper, a pinch of nutmeg, 1½ teaspoons of fresh marjoram and 120ml/4fl oz double cream. Process until all the ingredients are puréed. Butter 4 small individual soufflé dishes. Fill with the mushroom mixture. Bake in a *bain-marie*, in a preheated oven at 180°C/350°F/gas mark 4 for 30 minutes, or until the top is golden brown and firm. Serves 4.

Roast Pork on a Bed of Potatoes

Peel 3 garlic cloves and cut in thin slivers. With the point of a knife make several holes in a 1.8kg/4lb pork roast to insert the garlic. Rub the pork with 2 tablespoons soy sauce mixed with ½ tablespoon sesame oil. Sprinkle the pork with coarse salt and freshly ground pepper. Peel and thinly slice 5 large potatoes. Oil the bottom of a baking pan. Cover the bottom of the pan with the potatoes. Sprinkle with salt and pepper and 2 tablespoons chopped rosemary. Place the roast pork on top. Add 225ml/8fl oz of chicken bouillon to the pan and bake in a 180°C/350°F/gas mark 4 oven for 1 hour. Add more bouillon if necessary. Remove from the oven and cool for 10 minutes before slicing. Serve with the potatoes. Serves 8.

CHAPTER
FOUR

SoHo

Juliette was born on 2 June 1959. "Another girl!" Jimmy muttered when he saw her, "But so beautiful." And he was right. Juliette was the most beautiful new-born baby I had ever seen. We sent pictures of the two girls home to Paris. In response Mira, my stepfather, sent us tickets to come to Paris to spend the summer with them.

A few days after Juliette was born Suzanne Chen, my Chinese friend, came to visit to see the new baby.

"Lovely baby," she said, "but I have to talk to you both. Juliette," she said, "has an eye problem. She has what we call nystagmus. Her eyes roam without focusing. I don't know how much she can or will see. It could be temporary, but I'm not sure. I want to send you to a friend with whom I studied. He's a great specialist."

We were crushed, worried to death. Was she blind? Would she ever see? What was nystagmus?

The next few days were difficult. Suzanne made all the appointments and it was confirmed that Juliette had nystagmus, a defect of the optic nerve. It was with a heavy heart that we all left for Paris.

The summer went quickly. Marianne was learning French words and Juliette, despite her eye problem, was developing into a round, lovely, smiling baby. My relationship with my mother was, for the first time in years, calm and normal.

In the autumn, back in New York, I began to look for a new teaching job. In late September I was hired to teach French by the Browning School for Boys. To my surprise on my first day of school I found out that I was the only woman amongst the twenty-seven male staff! I spent four delightful years there.

In 1961, pregnant once again, we moved to an old house on 19th Street, and Cecile, our third daughter, was born on 15 September of that year. Frau Zeimnitz wasn't too happy to be looking after three children and soon she left us. Despite the problem we had finding another nanny, life seemed wonderful.

Cecile was quite different from the other two. She was fair like Jim, with enormous blue-green eyes and very blond hair. The following summer we went to East Hampton for a month. My friend Elisabeth Fonseca had also given birth to a little girl, Isabelle. Isabelle and Cecile were complete opposites. As fair as Cecile was, Isabelle was dark, with skin the colour of a ripe peach. Every day Elisabeth and I would take our children to the beach. One morning I dozed on the beach for a second and lost track of Cecile. Screams from the older children woke me up. Cecile was being rolled in a wave. I ran and caught her up, and for a few seconds thought all was lost. But Cecile was all right, except that from that day on she would not go near the water.

For Christmas that year we went once again to visit my mother-in-law. The weather was warm and every day we went to the beach. Cecile would join us all dressed up in a winter coat, socks and shoes. She would sit under a palm tree and watch the other children play and bathe. I tried several times to convince her that the water was not dangerous and that I would be holding her all the time. Cecile was a very serious and determined child. Nothing would move her if she did not want to be moved. At my mother-in-law's suggestion I stopped badgering her. Several days later I suddenly saw Cecile walk towards the water, and she slowly went in still wearing her coat and shoes. She had conquered her fear on her own terms. This trait would govern all her future actions. From that day on Cecile loved the water and became an excellent swimmer.

When Cecile turned three, having problems with nannies, I put her in a day nursery close to home. Marianne and Juliette went to a public school near the house, and we would all meet again at three o'clock.

At home I spoke French to the children and Jimmy spoke English. Marianne was totally bilingual, as was Juliette. However, between them they spoke English. One day Cecile came home, stood in front of me and declared as seriously as a three-year-old can "I am not French, I am an American. I will never speak French."

The next day I went to see her teacher to ask what had happened in school for Cecile to be so determined not to speak French with me.

"She has an accent when she speaks English," Mrs Hamburger, her teacher, told me. "The children made fun of her way of pronouncing *th*. She says *ze*, like *ze* mother, or *ze* school."

I realized then that Cecile, and not my other children, had picked up my accent. I cannot to this day pronounce *the* correctly. Mine comes out as *fe*!

Cecile kept to her word. In school, and later in college, she opted for Spanish and Chinese.

In early 1965 I found myself pregnant again, and this time the school was quite angry with me. They did not think that a pregnant woman should be around growing boys. At that time no law had been passed to protect pregnant woman from being fired and the school, to my chagrin, let me go.

Our children were growing, Juliette's eye problems had improved, and Jimmy was very successful in his work. With my job we had been financially secure, but now I was worried that with four children I would have a problem not only finding another job, but also a nanny. Thomas was born on 24 November 1965, Thanksgiving Day.

Three months later I was hired by Hofstra University to teach French to their third year students.

The house on 19th Street was now too small for our growing family, so Jimmy and I decided to look for somewhere bigger. One day a real estate agent I knew called and said she had a house that she thought I would like. She could not accompany us to see it so she handed me the key and an address, and said I could return the keys the following week.

That weekend Jimmy and I went downtown to Sullivan Street, below Houston Street, to take a look. It was twice as wide as our house on 19th Street, with four storeys and an immense garden. I stood in awe in the enormous living room; it had twelve-foot-high ceilings and two fireplaces. I could see myself sitting in front of a roaring fire reading a favourite novel. As for Jimmy, it was a dream: an enormous space with lots of light. We returned several times. I loved the house, I saw the garden's potential and thought that my four young children would love it too. But the house had no heating and no kitchen, and the rest of it was a wreck. However, we were determined to buy it. "Don't worry," Jimmy said, "Toothless and I will make it work."

"Toothless" was the nickname we had given to a jack of all trades we had met a few summers before. For two summers in a row we had rented an old farmhouse in Hunterdon County, New Jersey, for a month. Whenever anything went wrong in the house, which was every other day, we would call our landlord's ex-husband. His name was Bob but we called him Toothless because he lacked front teeth. Toothless had served in the merchant marines and was very clever at fixing things without spending a great deal of money. We had become good friends (he adored my cooking), so when we moved to 19th Street in 1961 he agreed to help us fix the house. He built a kitchen and painted the house with Jimmy. When Jimmy called him with a promise of a steady job for a few months (plus my cooking), he agreed to come and help rebuild the new house.

As I was now very busy packing and teachings I needed a good live-in help. This is when Gladys came into our lives and our problems with nannies were over. Gladys came from the South. She was a young, plump woman of about twenty-eight, full of joy and laughter. My children loved her, especially Marianne. Gladys would spend hours combing her hair and telling her stories about her boyfriends. I was content that my children were happy, and that I now had time to explore our new neighbourhood.

Sullivan Street, our part of Sullivan Street that is, began at Houston Street and went all the way to Broome. Houston is a large avenue which starts at the East River and crosses Manhattan just below Bleecker Street. Houston divided the neighbourhood in two: south of Houston — SoHo — was Italian working class, and north of Houston was where established urban professionals lived in the MacDougal-Sullivan Gardens district, concealed behind rows of 1920's Federal-style town houses.

Our street, along with Thompson Street and West Broadway, was part of an Italian enclave that included a block and a half of MacDougal Street. My intimacy with the neighbourhood began even as lawyers were preparing to complete on our house. I walked down Sullivan Street and Thompson Street, looking at the few stores that existed and observing my soon-to-be neighbours. The street was all Italian and mostly aging. The younger generations had long ago moved to

Brooklyn or Queens, or to the outer suburbs. There were also a few Portuguese families living in two or three buildings near Thompson Street. On Sullivan Street, between Houston and Prince, was a *latticini*, an Italian milk and cheese store. The aroma of freshly made mozzarella and smoked mozzarella wafted through the street. As a new arrival, and with the idea that I should become known to the street, I bought a fresh mozzarella home for our dinner every night. Joe, the owner, also sold Parmesan, olive oil, olives, ricotta and a few staples. Next door to Joe's was a candy store usually filled with Italian teenagers chatting or sipping sodas and doing nothing, at least this is how it seemed to me. Bruno's Bakery was next door. The bakery sold every Italian pastry I had tasted in Italy plus Italian bread and crackers. Opposite was the enormous, undistinguished front of the parish Church of St Anthony. The church, run by the Franciscan Friars, had a grey granite façade done in a style that Jimmy called Italianate Grotesque.

On Sundays, Jimmy and I would enjoy a slow walk down Sullivan Street to take in the scene. The church was filled with couples in their best Sunday clothes. Women in long black silk dresses, with old fashioned hats perched on their teased hair. The younger women were more stylish, in bright coloured dresses. None were wearing slacks. After mass, the women gathered to chat in groups of two or three outside the church, while their husbands, in shiny electric blue or pale grey suits, stood on the other side of the street in front of Bruno's bakery. They all carried boxes of pastries. I imagined

105

that the boxes were filled with *cannolli* stuffed with a thick sweet cream, or *babas* soaked in rum for their Sunday meal.

On the corner of Sullivan and Prince the pattern was repeated with the Portuguese, but this time only by men. The rest of the week the Church of St Anthony was closed, except for bingo night on Thursdays in the church's basement. Near the church were a group of small stores, one selling homemade sausages, another dealt in haberdashery. An uninviting café with tables and chairs and a bar was also nearby. Eventually I would learn that this was actually a social club called the Saxon Knights.

Towards the corner at Prince Street, was a butcher's shop, and what was extraordinary about it was that the butcher was a woman. Catherine Carnevari was big, tall and very strong. I often saw Catherine carrying in a whole side of beef as if it were a bouquet of roses. The store was large, with white tiles covering the walls and floor, and there were always three or four older women sitting on chairs near a table covered with newspapers, chatting about the neighbourhood, their kids or the latest love triangle. When we moved, I soon joined the women and sat on a chair listening to their chatter. I learned that Catherine was married to a sanitation man half her size; that he was afraid of her and that she, they whispered when she was not listening, beat him quite often, especially when he came home drunk. Five years later he died in mysterious circumstances. The whole neighbourhood, including me, went to the funeral. Catherine looked even larger dressed all in black. Later that year, to the chagrin of all the women in the neighbourhood, Catherine sold the store to a French man who turned it into a pastry shop and café.

At the corner of Prince and Sullivan was a large luncheonette, Vinnie's Coffee Shop. Vinnie ran the luncheonette with Maria, his mother, who did all the cooking. The white Formica tables were turning dirty yellow with age. At lunch Vinnie's was full of men and women from the surrounding blocks eating Maria's famous meatball sandwich drowned in spicy tomato sauce, or her *spaghetti marinara* along with cold beer.

In front of our house, which was in the middle of the block, stood De Pauli's grocery store. Just before we moved in, I started to go to De Pauli's to buy sandwiches for our lunch if Maria's was too crowded. I loved the store, which had been founded by Willy De Pauli's grandfather at the turn of the century. Willy was a tall, thin, slightly balding man with a mournful expression. He never really smiled, but he was the nicest man in my new neighbourhood. The store was generous, fitted with wood-panelled walls and countless storage cabinets with wood-framed glass doors, full of hundreds of different types of pasta. Willy sold sandwiches filled with thin slices of mortadella, ham or cheese on puffy Italian bread. Women would come in, buy a pound of pasta for dinner and would say to Willy, "I want 5-22-74-5." I wondered what these numbers were. Once we'd moved in and I felt more secure about my standing with him, I asked Willy what these numbers were for? His answer was, "Not for you. Don't ask! They gamble." And this was all I could get out of him.

Next to De Pauli's was Freddie's luncheonette and a Chinese laundry. The laundry was run by a young couple, the Wongs, who had two young children. When Thomas was a toddler he befriended the children, and I often asked them to come and play with him. They always sat on our stoop to play, refusing to come into our house. Tina, the little girl, was beautiful. I was sure Thomas had a crush on her. And so for the following three years, until he went to Kindergarten, Thomas could be found sitting on our stoop with the other kids playing with toy cars or stoop ball.

The remaining block was filled with tenements. Then at the corner of Sullivan and Spring was an Italian restaurant, the Napoli, run by three sisters. The Napoli was the restaurant where you took your Sullivan Street parents for Sunday dinner if you had moved out to the suburbs. It had a rust-coloured stucco façade and illuminated neon beer signs in the window. At the front of the restaurant was a narrow bar packed with men with heavy gold chains hanging around their necks, drinking beer and arguing in loud voices. In the back was a small dining room. By early evening, the restaurant was full. The menu, which changed daily, was written on a blackboard, and no one asked for the written menu. (I asked for a menu on my first visit and got a dirty look from the waitress; I never did it again.) Thursdays were my favourite. On Thursdays you could have a plate of tender, succulent tripe in a rich tomato sauce served with lots of hot garlic bread to mop it up.

The chicken was also good, and so were the mussels on Fridays. My favourite vegetable was the sautéd *escarole* with thick slices of tender garlic.

Thompson Street, around the corner, was very different, as it had very few stores. There was a Portuguese Deli at the corner of Thompson and Prince, a sausage store in the middle of the block, then at the corner of Thompson and Spring was a shop front which read the Village Community Problem Center. The people who ran it were trying to help old Italian families who had battles with their landlords, or young mothers whose children had problems either with the police or at school.

But the great attraction of Thompson Street was Mary Finelli's Candy store. Mary was born and raised on Thompson Street. At four o'clock after school her store would be filled with screaming children buying sweets for a few pennies. Mary controlled the shouting with a tough teacher's voice and had strict rules. You were not allowed to buy more than two types of sweets. The children often tried, going out of the store and coming back in asking to buy two more. Mary was never fooled, and the children adored her.

In the middle of the block on Prince Street between Thompson and West Broadway was the Vesuvio Bakery, run by a small man with slicked-down black hair called Tony Dapolito. He looked like an Italian lover from movies of the thirties. I was told by the real estate agent who had sold us the house that Tony Dapolito was the de facto Mayor of South Village, but his real power base was the territory between West Broadway and Sixth

Avenue. Tony sold several different breads and crunchy breadsticks. The best ones were hard dried toasts called *pizzelli* which were used for dipping in soup or for absorbing hot Italian tomato sauce. I first experienced them at Napoli where they were served with mussels *marinara* on Fridays. I wanted to be in Tony Dapolito's good graces, so every afternoon on my way back from work, I bought these sublime toasts, either peppered or plain, or some golden, crunchy breadsticks to take with me to work the next day.

It was impossible for a young struggling couple like Jimmy and I to carry a mortgage on the new house while still paying the rent on 19th Street, not to mention paying Toothless and buying materials to redo the new house. So we decided to move into our Sullivan Street house immediately. I started to pack our household possessions. Naima my sister-in-law helped, and so did Toothless. I packed our clothes in large wardrobe boxes and everyone, including the movers, laughed at me as I wrote "close" on each box. We moved into an empty house that had only a single toilet and one wash basin on the first floor. There was no kitchen and no bathroom. The radiators barely got warm from a frail steam heating system whose boiler was in the house of our next-door neighbours, the Brods, who bought their house at the same time as we did. Naturally they wanted us to get a new heating system immediately. This was going to be expensive, but it had to be done, so our first priority was to find a real plumber rather than Toothless. I also had other worries:

"How do we live in this empty house with four children, the youngest only eighteen months old?" I asked Jimmy. "I don't think we can do it!"

"Yes we can. We'll put our bed in the living room and put the children's mattresses on the floor next to us. We'll buy a microwave oven to heat breakfast, an electric kettle for tea, paper plates and cups, and for dinner we will go out and explore all the local restaurants. No problem, you'll see."

I took two weeks off from Hofstra University to pack and organize the move, but it was only when we had moved that the problems really started.

Thomas was crawling all over the place, and the floor was not the best place for him. Toothless had removed the linoleum that had covered the stairway, exposing the nails. While he removed the nails on the three flights of stairs, we had to watch Thomas like hawks. Gladys could do little else but keep an eye on him. Then we had to teach him how to climb the steps, getting him to sit on the first step then slide down on his bottom, just in case he escaped us. Finally he succeeded, and with great peals of laughter he reached the lowest floor.

The next problem was how to wash ourselves and our four children. The three girls went to school every day and couldn't go looking like dirty urchins. How do you wash kids with no hot water, no shower, and no bathroom?

I made a list of all our friends who lived within a ten-block radius and begged. Could we impose upon them once a week, all six of us, to come and take showers?

I was delighted by their responses — they all came to the rescue. So on Mondays we bathed at Elisabeth Fonseca's house; on Tuesdays at the Ghents; Wednesday was bad because no one could have us, but on Thursdays and Fridays we went to my neighbour, Mrs. Brod, and on the weekends to my in-laws. After one month I was afraid that I had used all my friends' goodwill and started to apologize profusely. They all told me not to worry, and soon we found a plumber who promised that within a month the top floor bathroom would be finished.

Having established a routine for ourselves and the children, after my two weeks' leave I was ready to go back to teaching.

The morning I was to return to work I got up very quietly and, since we were all sleeping in one room, I decided I would have a coffee across the street at Freddie's luncheonette. As I entered I looked around. I was astonished by the crowd at the counter. I was the only woman in the place. Most of the men looked as if they were construction workers, and there were two policemen in uniform. They were all drinking beer or hard liquor and wine. Freddie's was a bar, not a luncheonette! Freddie — I assumed it was Freddie himself behind the bar — was short and plump, with very thick glasses. He looked at me and said in a very polite but gruff voice:

"What you want?"

"Could I have a cup of coffee and an English muffin?"

"I haven't served a cup of coffee in twenty years! Who are you? Where do you live?"

"Across the street at 114, in the big house."

Suddenly one of the men drinking called to me: "Have a drink . . . on me . . . c'mon beautiful, have a drink."

I was about to leave when Freddie took my side and said: "Leave the lady alone."

Suddenly all the men were silent and looked sheepishly at Freddie.

"Today I can't give you any coffee lady, but tell me what you want every day and at what time. It'll be here for you."

"I go to work Monday, Wednesday and Friday. Could I have coffee and an English muffin?"

"You got it!" Freddie said with a grimace that was a smile.

And so three times a week at six o'clock in the morning, my coffee and an English muffin would be waiting for me. The men at the counter now greeted me with a warm "Hi". Freddie never allowed them to be rude or familiar with me. A few days later, wanting to thank him for his kindness, I went into his luncheonette in the early afternoon. To my surprise, the scene had radically changed. The counter was packed with women drinking soda or juices. Freddie's wife, Marie, was now behind the counter chatting with the women. The opposite of Freddie, Marie was a tall, plump woman with greyish hair and a sweet smile. Every afternoon, just before school let out, the women would gather in the luncheonette while Marie would hold court, giving advice on numerous subjects from how to make a pasta recipe to what to do when your daughter was dating someone you did not like because he was not Italian. Some of the women, I also learned, were widows, or older women whose husbands were playing "*bacci*", the Italian ball game, in special bars on MacDougal Street or drinking espressos at their social club. The luncheonette was a sort of social club for the women who had nowhere else to go.

Marie had two children, a son and a daughter. The daughter was married and lived across the street from the luncheonette. Their son Andy was a problem, as I had heard from sitting in the butcher's store. He took drugs and was often drunk. Often one could see him walking down Sullivan Street muttering to himself, while the old ladies would shake their heads in disgust. Years later when both Marie and Freddie died and the luncheonette was sold to become a beauty salon, the old ladies lost their meeting place. Some died; others left the street to join their children in Queens, and a few elected the beauty salon as their new meeting place because the salon was run by a beautiful young Italian woman, Pat, who knew everyone on the street. Pat and I later became good friends, and when she decided to move her beauty salon two doors down, Jimmy designed it for her.

In the first month of living in the house we resolved the problem of feeding the family. On Mondays, Wednesdays and Fridays I sent all four children to

Luigi's Restaurant at the corner of Prince and Sullivan, where Luigi's wife would take care of them. The restaurant was a long dark room with banquettes on both sides. At the front there was a bar and at around five it was always filled with workers having a drink before heading home. Most nights the children ate pasta, meat balls and salad. Jimmy and I ate sandwiches in the living room. The other two days and on weekends I cooked in the fireplace. I used a Hibachi, a small Japanese barbecue set in the hearth. In fact I became quite expert at cooking in the fireplace. We had lived in Italy, in Umbria, where cooking in the fireplace was commonplace. For example, veal chops were marinated in a mixture of lemon juice, olive oil and herbs for a couple of hours, then grilled over hot coals. I also learned what vegetables would cook easily and quickly. Aubergines thinly sliced and brushed with olive oil cooked in a few minutes, as did fresh *shiitake* or portobello mushrooms. Grated carrots tossed with lemony vinaigrette made a delicious salad, and frozen, tiny green peas could be heated in the microwave. That month we ate a lot of hamburgers, pork chops and veal chops.

Slowly the house started to take shape. On weekends we both worked side by side with Toothless. I painted the children's bathroom, learned how to tape plasterboard and remove linoleum with a blow torch. The children's room was finally finished and they all moved to the top floor.

One Saturday, I sanded the front door and painted it with glossy black paint. To my horror, the next morning the front door was all scratched and my work was destroyed. I was very upset and decided to repaint it, and try to catch who had done it. But since I had no time until the following weekend, I had to wait. Jimmy and I now slept alone in the living room, and one night, unable to sleep, still quite upset by the front door incident, I got up and walked towards the window to look out at the street, silent and empty. Suddenly I saw a young boy running towards our house, a rag in his hand. He climbed the stoop, lit the rag with a match and was about to run down when in an instant I was outside in my nightgown and grabbed him by the hair. I pushed away the furiously burning rag soaked with gasoline and started screaming, shaking him like a rag doll.

"Who are you? What's your name? Who sent you? I'll call the police . . ."

A few minutes later, I found myself surrounded by about 10 women. Still holding the boy by the hair I kept screaming:

"Who's your mother? Where is she? Where do you live? What's your name? Answer or I will call the police."

The boy slowly pointed to one of the women standing by.

I dragged the child over to her.

"Is he yours?"

She whispered "yes."

For a second I did not know what to do. Should I call the police? I was still in my nightgown so I made a quick decision.

"Take him home. If I see him within ten feet of my house, I will file a complaint. Now tell me where you live."

"Two houses down," she answered, taking the boy by the arm. "Don't worry, it won't happen again."

The next morning I told Toothless what had happened. He sat me down and said, "Let me tell you about the street. This is Mafia territory. You have invaded their turf and they don't know who you are. They are very good people, family people; they just don't want someone not Italian living here."

As I was about to protest that we too were a hard-working family, he shook his head and continued: "Freddie, who is so nice to you, collects the money for the number games. Have you seen the black limousine parked in the street on Friday nights? They come to collect it. Willy takes down the numbers, collects the money and gives it to Freddie. You know the social club down the street? That's where they gather and discuss their affairs. You are intruding. Give them time. The best thing you did was to not call the police."

The next day, on my way home from work, I stopped at the social club and sat down at one of the empty tables. A few men were playing cards; they looked baffled to see me there. A fat, middle-aged man stood up and walked towards me. He must be the owner, I thought, and so I asked him for a coffee.

"We don't serve coffee."

"A glass of juice, any kind of juice?"

"No juice! We serve nothing."

This was clearly not Freddie's luncheonette. No one here was going to acknowledge my presence, let alone accommodate me. The man walked away so I sat there silently; then I started to talk.

"I am the new owner of 114 . . . I am French and we have four children . . . I work as a teacher and my husband is an architect . . ." (No answer, no sign that any one was listening) "I work hard, so does he. We are not rich . . . I chose this neighbourhood because I had an Italian wet nurse . . . My first words were Italian . . ." (Still no reaction) "and I love our house. We feel so safe . . . like in a village. I want my children to grow up here."

As I got no reaction, I stood up and left, saddened.

That night I told Jimmy what I'd done and how I'd failed.

"Don't worry. You heard what Toothless said: they'll get used to us."

For the next few weeks nothing happened. Our bedroom was finished, so we moved up to our floor. Now we had two bathrooms and no need to bother our friends. The next task was to create a kitchen out of the former outhouse. Toothless had found an old Italian tile setter in the neighbourhood, and so Jimmy ordered a ton of sand for the dining room and kitchen.

A few days later at 7a.m. the front doorbell rang. I ran to open the door to a man holding papers.

"Rossant? I have your sand. Please sign here."

Once I'd signed, I saw the truck turn around and dump one ton of sand on the sidewalk.

"But you can't do that. It has to be in bags! How will we bring it in?"

"Lady, this is not my problem, but a word of advice: if you don't want a ticket, start bringing it in right away."

I woke up Jimmy and the three girls and Gladys and told them to take pots and pans, and together we would bring the sand in through the basement door.

We must have been a sight! The three little girls in their pyjamas, Thomas jumping on the sand, me in my dressing gown, Gladys in a short nightie and Jimmy the only one half-dressed. We formed a line. I filled the pots, Jimmy at the other end emptied them; in between the others passed along the pots and pans.

Within ten minutes we were surrounded by muscled young men from the neighbourhood lugging enormous containers, and in half an hour the sand was in the house. I made coffee for everyone, realizing that my speech at the social club had worked. We were now part of the street scene and had been accepted by the neighbourhood.

One morning in June, after we had been in the house six months, I saw that the street was crossed by high, illuminated arches every ten feet. I asked Willy what they were for. "Don't you know? It is for St Anthony's Fair. It lasts two weeks, with stands selling sausages, *zeppole* and pizza; there's gambling, and games like throwing baseballs or catching small fish. Officially the fair is run by the church, but really by Mike. You'll see him around collecting the fees for the church. You can't miss him; he's always screaming at everybody. Then, on the last day of the Fair there is a procession with a statue of the Virgin paraded up and down the street, her dress pinned with dollar bills. There's lots of music and a live band. You will love it!"

A few days later we saw a truck pulling an immense stand which stopped in front of our house. It was the first stand to be set up, and was owned by a man who sold sausages, sweetbreads and beer. Although he would appear with the fair for the next thirty years I never learned his name, but he was by far the most popular vendor in the fair. Short, skinny, adorned with a swooping white moustache and a white chef's hat perched on his bald head, a red handkerchief around his neck, he called people to his stand through a loudspeaker all day long and all night till two in the morning, making jokes and telling the crowds how wonderful his sausages were. Every morning his assistant, a fat, older man, sat on a chair near our house peeling a mountain of onions while the sausage man prepared his sweetbreads and sausages. The street was full of stinking rubbish. No one seemed to sweep up, and by the second day I was incensed. After work I went to him to complain about the rubbish all over the street and our stoop. He offered me a sausage sandwich. I was going to refuse, but the sausage sandwich looked tempting, so I accepted. I bit into the hot sweet sausage with great pleasure. I had to admit that it was excellent. I smiled and asked again if, at the end of the day, he could sweep all around his stand and my stoop. He promised he would do his best. But at the end of the first weekend, the rubbish was worse; people

120

sat on our stoop eating, dropping greasy onions on the steps. I hosed it down every morning, cursing the fair and everyone around. One day I decided to put sawdust on the steps, hoping that people wouldn't sit there. I was wrong. Nothing could stop them from sitting there. I called St Anthony's Church and spoke to the Father in charge of the fair. Father R. promised to help. However, after two days, the rubbish was overflowing, and despite my begging the stands in front of our house to sweep every night, it kept on accumulating.

A week after the fair was over, I went around the private houses on Sullivan Street and MacDougal and invited the owners to come and discuss the fair over a drink in our empty living room. I asked Father R. to join us too. My guests that night were Herbert Ferber, the sculptor, and his wife Edith, with whom we would become very good friends, the Brods, a young real estate man who had bought the house at the corner of Prince and a couple who live further down on Sullivan Street. We talked about the fair, the rubbish and the loud music. Father R. promised that the fair would be cleaner the following year. He would ask the Sanitation Department for more bins and he would see that each stand swept up around itself. But I wanted more. I wanted the fair to move somewhere else.

A few days later, as I entered our local liquor store its owner, Andrew, a middle-aged man who (as Willy told me) still lived with his mother and swept the church's steps every morning before attending mass, asked me to follow him into a small room behind the counter. He offered me a chair and he stood over me.

"You have to stop trying to move the fair and making trouble. You'll be hurt. People here love the fair. It has been here for fifty years. Who are you, and what gives you the right to make trouble?"

I stood there speechless. I loved the street and I couldn't fathom that the other people living on the street liked the fair. I looked up at Andrew. He was looking at me seriously, not smiling. I got up and left without a word.

Upset and worried, I went home and decided not to tell Jimmy about the lecture. The next morning I found a letter stuck in the front door. It was written in bad English and the gist of it was: If I continued trying to move the fair they would break my legs and set the house on fire. I will never know who *they* were. It could have been Andrew or some other people from the social club down the street. The warning was strong enough for me to cease and desist. I would have to live with the fair.

The following year our children decided to have a stand in front of the house and serve French *crêpes* with sugar or jam. Jimmy built them a small stand. I got a small electric hot plate and pan, and made the batter. Marianne, Juliette and Cecile spent the weekend making *crêpes*. They were so successful that Mike came around and told me I had to pay for the right to have a stand. I was incensed. I called Father R. and said that I refused to pay for using my own sidewalk! We finally agreed that I wouldn't pay Mike, but instead I'd make a donation to the Church. The following weekend our friend Calvin Trillin, passing by the fair, saw my three adorable little girls selling *crêpes*. He didn't realize they were our children, and the following week he had a story about them in the *New Yorker*.

As the years went by, I started to like the fair. It was like a small village fair filled with children screaming up and down the street, eating sweets, playing games. At the weekend I gave our children some money to eat and play at the fair. Sometimes, after work, I would walk through the fair and couldn't resist picking up a couple of *zeppole*, the round, fried dough rolled in sugar. They were hot, greasy, crunchy and delicious. On weekends I would invite friends for dinner and order *zeppole* from a fat lady at the corner of Sullivan and Spring to serve my guests as dessert. Yes, I was softening, but I still hated the fair's rubbish. I continued fighting with the church for thirty years. (In 2000 when we sold our house, the church, realizing that the street had changed and that the Italians had moved out to be replaced by more affluent residents, decided to eliminate the fair! I was astonished, and also somewhat sad and nostalgic. One more tradition that had made Sullivan Street so wonderful was disappearing just as we were moving out!)

When the house was finally finished, we decided to give a big party to celebrate. We had no furniture and no money to buy any, so Jimmy had a brilliant idea: to cover the windows and the round ornate plaster rosaces on the ceiling with Christmas lights and leave the place empty like the ballroom it resembled. We hired a three-piece Greek band and sent some three hundred invitations. Jimmy drew a picture showing the front of the whole house opening with the empty rooms behind. Was it because of Jimmy's drawing, or because people were curious about the house that everyone said yes? Jimmy was worried: Would the living-room floor hold with so many people dancing?

I had another worry: What to serve three hundred people? I went to see Catherine, the butcher, for advice. She suggested serving *cottechino*, a large fat sausage, with lentils. She would make me about twenty *cottechini*. "You can cook them in advance, slice them when cold and heat them on the night of the party in the oven. Very easy." Jimmy and I thought about what else to serve. We had very little money and so many guests!

"I know," Jimmy said, "let's go to the Bronx Terminal Market two days before the party."

We got up at five in the morning and drove to the Terminal Market near the Yankee Stadium. The market was clogged with enormous trucks loading and unloading. We parked and walked around. I saw cases of sweet peppers, red, orange and green, so we bought a case to make a *tricolore* salad in a lemony vinaigrette. Further down we found a case of endive to glaze with sugar.

Then I saw crates of tangerines and thought that they would make a great dessert placed in a large bowl in the centre of the table. Our shopping done, it was now 7.30 and we were famished. We stopped at a diner. It was packed with workers from South America eating

124

eggs, sausages, rice and beans. We ordered the same with a strong black Cuban coffee and had the best breakfast ever.

One day before the party, I also made Cairo-style *babaghanou* and *tarama* salad. I planned to have four different types of olives everywhere, and thin slices of Italian salami and mozzarella from Joe's store. I also made an enormous green salad. Catherine had suggested that I serve tiny *cannolli*, and said that she would talk to Bruno, the owner of the bakery down the street. She was sure he would give me a special price. I rented a few chairs for older people, dishes, forks and knives, plates, napkins and a table for the wine and sodas. I found an unemployed actor who agreed to serve the drinks.

Jimmy had decided that I should wear a Greek outfit, so we had gone shopping in a Greek store, near Third Avenue and 59th Street. We chose a dress in off-white cotton, long with lace around the waist. Jimmy also bought me a necklace and long earrings. A few days in advance, I told the neighbourhood that we were having a very large party to celebrate the end of the construction. Willy spread the word, and on the night of the party there were no cars on the street so that guests could park easily. For the first hour no one came and I got very nervous. The bartender tried to calm me down.

"You're in Manhattan," he said with a little smile. "People feel they have to be fashionably late." And as the Greek band played with gusto I, in my long Greek dress, stood waiting, thinking no one would come down to this neighbourhood!

Was I wrong! They arrived, it seemed to me, all at once. I greeted people, some I did not even know. We danced, and at ten o'clock I called people down to eat. And they ate and ate as Jimmy and I, still worrying about the floor, refilled the platters. We danced again, chatted, drank and had a great time. The party ended at three o'clock in the morning. No one in the street complained. Years later I would meet people I didn't recognise who would insist they knew us. "I was at a party at your house years ago. It was great and the food was fantastic!"

Mussels in Hot Tomato Sauce

Wash and clean 2 kilos/4lbs of mussels. Set aside. In a heavy saucepan heat 2 tablespoons olive oil. Add 4 tablespoons chopped parsley, 1 medium onion, finely chopped, I small carrot, scraped and finely chopped. Cook, stirring, for 5 minutes then add 3 garlic gloves, finely chopped, along with 150g/6oz chopped fresh basil. Mix well and cook for 4 minutes. Then add a 400g/14oz tin of whole tomatoes with the juice, some salt and chili flakes. Bring to a boil, lower the heat and simmer for 40 minutes or until the sauce has thickened. Set aside.

In a large saucepan melt 2 tablespoons of butter. When the butter is hot add 2 garlic cloves minced along with 5 tablespoons chopped parsley. Cook for 2 minutes, then add the mussels, mix well, cover and cook over a medium heat for 10 minutes, or until the mussels are all open. Then pour in the tomato sauce, mix well and serve with thick slices of warm Italian bread. Serves 8.

Broiled Veal Chops

Place 4 one-inch thick veal chops in a bowl. Mix together the juice of 1 lemon with 4 tablespoons olive oil, salt and pepper, 1 tablespoon rosemary, 1 tablespoon thyme and 1 tablespoon sage. Mix well. Pour over the veal chops and refrigerate for 1 hour, turning the veal chops several times. Broil over hot coals for 6 minutes on each side, or until the veal chops are golden brown. Serve with steamed corn and a salad. Serves 4.

Crêpes

In a food processor place 120g/4oz flour with 170ml/6fl oz milk, 3 eggs, 2 tablespoons melted butter, 1 tablespoon sugar and a pinch of salt. Process until all the ingredients are well mixed. Pour the batter into a bowl and let it stand for at least 1 hour.

Melt some butter in a rather flat skillet or crêpe pan. When the butter bubbles, pour in 3 tablespoons of batter and quickly tilt and rotate the pan until the batter covers the entire surface. When the edges begin to brown, turn the crêpe with a spatula and cook the other side for a few seconds. Slide the crêpe onto a dish. Sprinkle the crêpes with melted butter and sugar or with jam. If you wish to make several crêpes before serving them, cover with greaseproof paper and continue cooking. The crêpes can be kept warm in 130°C/225°F oven. Makes about 16 crêpes.

Cottechino with Lentils

Cottechino is a long, very fat garlic sausage. You could replace the cottechino with sweet Italian sausages. Use French or Italian green lentils for this dish.

Place 1 large cottechino in a saucepan. Cover with boiling water. Bring back to the boil, lower the heat and slowly cook for 30 minutes. Remove from the water and cool. Slice the cottechino in 1-inch slices and set aside while cooking the lentils. Place 300g/10oz of lentils in a saucepan. Add 1.2 litres/2 pints of chicken bouillon to cover the lentils. Add 1 bay leaf, salt and pepper to taste and 1 small whole onion. Bring to a boil, lower the heat to medium and cook until the lentils are tender. Cut 3 slices of smoked bacon in ½ inch pieces and sauté in a skillet until crisp. Drain on paper towel and add to the lentils. Then add 2 garlic cloves, thinly sliced, to the bacon fat. Sauté until golden brown. Add the garlic with half the bacon fat to the lentils. Mix well and correct the seasoning with salt and pepper. Heat the cottechino in the oven. Place the lentils on a serving platter, top with the sliced cottechino and serve with strong Dijon mustard. Serves 4 to 6.

Braised Fennel

Cut 1 inch off the top of 2 fennel bulbs. Then cut each bulb in two. Cut each half in thin slices. In a skillet heat 3 tablespoons butter. Add the fennel slices, salt and pepper and sauté the fennel, stirring often until they are lightly brown. Then add 150ml/5fl oz chicken stock and bring to a boil; lower the heat, cover and cook for 20 minutes. Then remove the cover, sprinkle with 1 tablespoon sugar and cook until the liquid has evaporated and the fennel is caramelized. Serve garnished with chopped coriander. Serves 4.

Mashed Potatoes with Anchovy

Wash 450g/1lb of potatoes. Place in a saucepan and cover with water. Bring to a boil, lower the heat to medium and cook until the potatoes are tender. Drain and cool. Peel the potatoes and pass through a ricer. In a small saucepan heat 2 tablespoons olive oil. Add 2 anchovy fillets cut in small pieces and cook stirring until the anchovies dissolve in the oil. Remove from the heat and add another 3 tablespoons olive oil. Mix well and add to the mashed potatoes. Add freshly ground pepper and more olive oil if necessary. Serves 4.

CHAPTER FIVE

Cooking with Colette

A year after Thomas was born I had been hired by Hofstra University to teach French Literature to future French teachers. Three times a week I would drive to the Hofstra Campus in Long Island early in the morning and come home at around four o'clock, just as my daughters were returning from school. One morning in January I woke up to six inches of snow. My car was an old jalopy and I didn't trust it in the snow and ice. For the first time I took the train to school. I arrived at Hempstead station, looking in vain for a taxicab to take me to Hofstra. Next to me stood a young woman wrapped in a fur coat. I asked her if she knew how I could get to the University from the station. I said I was late for my class and quite worried because I was a new teacher and still on trial. The young woman said, "I also teach at Hofstra, in the English department. Let's call for a taxi and share it. Don't worry; everyone will be late today, including the students. By the way, my name's Alice Trillin. I also live in Manhattan."

Alice was a beautiful young woman with light, wavy blond hair and large eyes. She talked rapidly and had an easy laugh. I liked her immediately, and very soon I invited her and her husband to dinner. Calvin, "Bud" to those close to him, was a writer for the *New Yorker*. He was charming, always joking and teasing us. He loved good food, and I loved having a guest who looked forward to my new way of cooking and my experiments.

When we first met, we had just moved into our Sullivan Street house and the Trillins were not far away on Grove Street — a pleasant walk through the village was all that separated us. I loved to have them for dinner; every time I found some interesting ingredient or a new Chinese restaurant, I would invite them over. Now feeling more secure and bold, I explored many small streets and back alleys in Chinatown. Chinatown was growing very fast, and I was never far behind. I discovered new restaurants, new markets, and was not afraid to ask questions and buy ingredients that were strange to me to try out at home. Sometimes it was with great results, sometimes with even greater disasters. I would call Suzanne and tell her about my disasters, and we both would laugh. Then she would explain how the Chinese cooked with whatever ingredients I had been too original with.

A few weeks before Abigail, Alice and Calvin's first daughter, was born, I called Alice:

"Alice, I just found a new vegetable in Chinatown. They call it water spinach; it's yummy. Come for dinner tomorrow night."

Come they did, and after we had eaten the appetizer — a cauliflower soup with blue cheese — Alice announced in an excited voice:

"I have to go home, I think the baby's coming. Bud, take me home."

Calvin got up and said in a hurt tone, "But I don't know what Colette's serving for the main course!"

We all laughed and I went to the kitchen and made the dinner "to go". I placed the roast quails that I had been going to serve with the water spinach in a container along with some sautéd water chestnuts, and said as I handed him the package:

"Don't worry; first babies take a long time. Here's what I would have served you. Good luck."

Abigail took another week to come, but the story of my care package ended up as a small story in one of Calvin's books, *Alice, Let's Eat*. He wrote: "One of my favorite New York cooks is a friend of ours named Colette Rossant . . . She defies Americanization and she is so far above frozen food that I always suspected that she may not keep ice cubes." The book was reviewed everywhere, and the *Wall Street Journal* used this quote from the book. All of a sudden the telephone started to ring and requests poured in for articles about food. The first call was from *Vogue* magazine, asking me to contribute to a series of articles by well-known cooks about dinners that had not gone as planned. I said yes right away; I certainly had the right material. Only a few weeks before, my husband had asked me to cook for one of his clients, a rich property developer with whom he was involved in a very large project. Jimmy had talked about me as a wonderful cook and the man had wanted to be invited to dinner.

"You have to go all out," Jimmy said, "it's very important for me."

Very carefully I planned the menu. I decided to make a cheese soufflé as a starter (serving a soufflé in 1968 was still exotic which is no longer the case today), half a young goat as the main course served with Chinese vegetables, and a purée spiced with black olives. For dessert I would make a beet pie. I had never made one before, but I thought it should be quite easy. I went shopping on Ninth Avenue in Asian stores, which I had recently discovered, and bought a baby goat. I cooked all day. The pie was beautiful, the colour of ruby; the goat was ready to be put in the oven, and the table was set. At 7p.m. I put my baby goat in the oven smeared with spices and French mustard. The developer, his wife and two of his associates arrived promptly and at eight we all sat down to what I thought would be a memorable dinner.

The first course went well. The golden soufflé had not collapsed and I thought that our guests were quite impressed. Once the plates were cleared, I took the baby goat out of the oven and tried to carve it. Impossible! I called Jimmy, who sharpened our knife and tried too. Still impossible. I had underestimated the cooking time. The goat was underdone and disaster threatened.

"Quickly go and pour more wine and give them fresh bread. Tell them that what I'm making has to be done at the last minute and might take some time."

I raised the oven temperature and waited ten more minutes. Still tough. This was not a baby goat I had bought, this was his grandmother! And so while they all drank more wine, I tore pieces of meat from the goat, cut it into tiny cubes. I wondered what I could make and decided on an *omelette*. I stuffed it with the goat cubes, lots of herbs, and garlic. I wasn't very sure what it would taste like but hoped that the herbs would enhance the dish. I also hoped that no one would think that the *omelette* was too unusual and bizarre. To this day I don't know what Jimmy thought of the dinner. All I know is that, as they left, the guests were full of praise, raving about my food and the very unusual *omelette*. Had they been too drunk to notice the taste of goat? The article about the goat was a success, more offers for articles came my way and thus my career as a food writer was born.

One day when Juliette, our second daughter, was in the fifth grade, she announced that many of her friends had formed "secret clubs". She wanted to form a secret club herself but had no ideas. What could she do? I suggested a cooking club. The idea arose from the fact that when I came home from work my children would be all around me, clamouring for my attention. I began to give them jobs to do in the kitchen. I taught them how to peel vegetables, stir the sauces, and so on. I told Juliette to select a few friends, and invite them to our house one Saturday a month to learn how to cook one dish that they would eat for lunch, and another they would take home. Juliette would charge a quarter. She was enthusiastic and came back the next day triumphant, saying that she had four new friends who

134

would join us at the end of the week for the first meeting of the secret cooking club.

That first Saturday, I had in my kitchen five little girls eagerly waiting to be taught how to cook. I was scared. It is one thing to show your child how to separate an egg, but now I had children I didn't really know who looked at me eagerly, probably expecting a miracle that in one day they would know how to cook!

I had decided that each child would make *quiches* for lunch and some small apple pies to take home. And so I gave each child a bowl, a wooden spoon, a knife, flour, etc. I went from child to child teaching each how to measure, wiping the spills and praying that the dough would work. We made the dough that I call "never fail dough", the one that my own grandmother had taught me as a little girl in Egypt. I taught the girls how to break eggs and separate the yolks from whites, allowing the white to slide through their hands into the bowl. "Disgusting," said one little girl, laughing as the yolk also fell in the bowl and I picked it up with my hands. We beat the yolks with cream, grated some Swiss cheese, rolled the dough and lined the pie plates with the dough. We beat the whites and folded the beaten whites into the yolks. Soon the *quiches* were assembled and the five little girls, trembling with excitement, each placed their *quiche* in the oven. While they baked, we made a French open apple pie with the remaining dough. The children were going to take the uncooked apple pies home to bake them there.

When the *quiches* were ready we all sat around the table and ate. For most of the children this was their first taste of *quiche*. "I love it," cried one of the girls. This was followed by grunts of approval from the other children. The day had been a great success. Juliette was happy, and as they left the house she handed them the recipes of what they had made. I was exhausted, but pleased to see the smile of contentment on my little girl's face.

On Monday when Juliette returned from school she announced that other girls in the class, having learned how much fun the five friends had had, wanted to join the club.

"Can I invite other friends to come?" Juliette asked.

I didn't think I could afford to have so many children. At a quarter per child I would quickly go broke. Also, more than five would be too many to handle. I said to Juliette:

"We'll see next month. Maybe the ones who want to join now will have forgotten about your secret club. You can invite the same children to come back." But time did nothing to dull their enthusiasm. By the end of April, about twenty mothers had called me to ask if their children could join the club. "I hear that you really teach them how to cook and that they loved it. I never learned anything from *my* mother. She never taught me! I am such a bad cook . . . I really wish you would reconsider and take my daughter."

One night our friend, Alan Buchsbaum, came by. Alan was an architect and graphic designer, and above all my best friend. What we had in common was cooking as he was one of the best cooks I knew in New

York. He and I often cooked together. I told him of my predicament. "What should I do?" I asked.

"I know. Let's make it a *real* cooking school. You can charge for teaching, and teach every Saturday morning. I'll design a flyer and you can send it to all the private schools. Parents have no idea of what to do with their children on a Saturday. You'll be a godsend to the mothers."

And true to his word, Alan made a flyer announcing COLETTE'S COOKING SCHOOL. We calculated how much the food and utensils would cost and decided what to charge the parents. We mailed the flyer to all the private schools.

The school would start the first Saturday in June, when private schools began their summer vacation. Alan also secretly sent the flyer to Corky Pollan, *New York Magazine*'s Best Bet's editor. She mentioned the cooking school in her column and we received hundreds of calls. This time it was not only girls who wanted to come, but boys too. I decided that we would have three sessions a week. Each session would have eight kids: four boys and four girls. I also had to make some rules. The children had to be at least eight, and tall enough to look into a saucepan without going on tiptoe. A few days before the first class I had a call from the *New York Times*, who had heard about the school and wanted to send a reporter. I tried to dissuade them from coming on the first day. Couldn't they wait? No, was the answer. As the parents dropped their children at our house a reporter roamed among them, asking questions.

We were all in the dining room. Each child had a wooden chopping board, a small knife, wooden spoons, bowls, and so on. For the first session, as I knew I had a reporter looking on, I decided to stick with the same dishes we had made at Juliette's first cooking club meeting. We made eight *quiches*, and eight apple pies. To my relief the *quiches* came out of the oven golden brown. The kids loved them; even the little girl who kept on saying "I hate eggs" ate it with relish.

It was around that time that my stepfather announced that the two of them would come to visit us that summer. Mira wanted to travel around the United States with my mother, and also spend some time with us. I was delighted.

A week before their arrival, my mother called saying that their trip would be delayed as Mira had pneumonia. I was very upset and kept calling home to see how he was. Two weeks later he died. I was heartbroken; I had loved him as if he had been my father.

In one of my Saturday classes was the daughter of a television producer. He came to watch one day, and suggested that we make a pilot and present it to PBS. PBS loved the idea but refused to put up the money, so he turned to Warren Steibel, a well-known television producer who produced William Buckley's *Firing Line*, a political talk show filmed in South Carolina.

Warren Steibel decided to present the idea to South Carolina Public Television, which took on the sponsorship of the show. As the new school year had started by this time and I was back teaching, we decided that we would start filming the show in July.

But what would I do with my four children?

It was then that my mother wrote saying that she was lonely, and that she wanted to come and live in New York, not with us but near us. She said she would love to help with the children. I found my mother an apartment across the street from us, and after she had settled down and got used to New York, Warren Steibel organized the filming of the show.

He flew me to Columbia to start filming. The plan was to do twelve episodes. Four boys and four girls would join me in each episode, and each show would be geared to a different age group, ending with a Christmas dinner cooked by older children.

Warren put me on South Carolina public radio, asking children to come to the studio to an interview for a cooking show. The response was overwhelming; hundreds of children swarmed into the radio station. Warren refused to let me see any of the children, saying that the element of surprise as I met them on the set would make for a better television show. We decided together that the first episode would be about dough, pies, cracking eggs, etc. The first shoot went well, although Warren had failed to factor in that the children were Southerners with a heavy southern drawl, and I had a French accent. The dialogue between the children and me was as funny as an Abbott & Costello sketch. I dimly understood what they were saying and they barely understood me, but we managed.

139

It was also quite difficult to find the ingredients for the show. Columbia was not New York, after all. No artichokes, no really fresh vegetables, and the only salad available was iceberg lettuce. For every show we had to scramble for ingredients; sometimes they were flown in from New York, at other times we appealed to the public. On one of the shows we were going to make a watercress soup. The crew was unable to find any. Watercress, I was told, was not available in Columbia. "Impossible," I said, "watercress grows everywhere." So I went on the air asking people who lived in the suburbs of Columbia, and who had a brook in their backyard, to look for wild watercress, describing the small green leaves as clearly as possible. The next day we had a line of cars and trucks filled with watercress arriving at the studio. We made the soup and the whole town of Columbia got hooked on watercress soup!

For the last episode the average age of the children was fifteen, and I had decided that I would teach them how to prepare and roast a goose. We had the usual problem: no geese were available in Columbia. Warren decided that he would order them in from New York. A day before filming, we received nine geese. I would roast one and place it in the set's oven. The next day each child prepared their own. As we prepared the geese and chatted about Christmas presents and what the children ate for their Christmas dinners (not one of them had ever had or even seen a goose before! Ham or turkey was what they ate), the aroma of the cooked goose wafted through the studio. When we had finished preparing the geese, I went to the oven and removed the cooked goose. Usually, as I set prepared dishes on the table, Warren would scream "cut" and the children would then grab what they had prepared. This time Warren forgot to say "cut". As I set the goose on the table, everyone in the studio rushed to the table to get a taste of the goose, fighting with the children. All of that went on the tape!

In September the show was aired on PBS stations around the country, and the *New York Times* television critic loved it, calling it a "a very funny show, one that children and parents should watch together".

I was now quite busy teaching at Hofstra, running the cooking school, and writing articles on food. One day Alan called me to invite me to lunch with a friend of his who wanted to meet me. Barbara Plummer was, I found out midway through the lunch, the senior editor at Scribner's. She asked me to talk about my ideas for a cookbook for children. A cookbook for children? I looked at Alan who looked the other way. What had he told her? Was I to talk about a book I hadn't even thought about? So I invented a book on the spot. Looking up at Barbara I said: "Yes, I want to write a cookbook for children based on my cooking school. The book would start with desserts and end up with vegetables. I'll tell the story about how I learned to cook. The recipes will be simple, but real. There will be no 'mud pies'! And I think Jimmy should illustrate the book with line drawings. Children will love them."

Barbara loved the idea, and a month later I received a contract. I was in a state of panic. Write a book? I didn't know how or where to begin. I couldn't type, I couldn't spell, and at that time there were no computers to help you along. What was I going to do? I called my friend Lorraine Davis, an editor at *Vogue*. Lorraine had assigned me my first story and remained a staunch supporter. "Very easy," she said. "Buy a tape recorder, sit down and talk into the microphone. Then give the tapes to someone to type up. Read them, correct the recipes, and send me the manuscript. I'll edit it. You're a story-teller, so don't worry."

I didn't know how I was going to write with the children out of school and needing my constant supervision. It was July, so Elisabeth Fonseca, my friend, suggested that I send the children to her house in East Hampton, along with Lucy, our new housekeeper. I would come on the weekends and write all week.

Lucy was my gift from the gods. Gladys had stayed with us until the house was finished, and then announced that she was leaving us to get married. We were sad to lose her but happy for her. Now I needed someone who would live in, look after the children, and help me run the big house. I had heard through friends that there was a family of Columbian women looking for work. Was I interested? I was. So one day Lucy came to our house. Lucy was a tall, round woman with an easy smile and a warm embrace. She didn't speak a word of English and my Spanish was elementary, but we understood one another, mixing words of Spanish, French and Italian.

As soon as the children were settled in Elisabeth's guest house, I worked full time for two months, and then used every free moment to work through the winter months too. Jimmy read the manuscript and did the drawings. He drew funny cartoons, creating a figure that was neither a boy nor a girl, so that both could identify with the main character of the story. By the spring the book was finished, and I sent the manuscript to Lorraine Davis. She loved it and went to work editing the book.

At around this time I met Rita Reinhardt, the widow of the artist Ad Reinhardt. She came to me with a proposition. She was involved with a project called Art Park. Earl Brydges, State Senator from Lewiston near Buffalo, had decided to put his town on the map by creating an art park there. The idea was that art should be a performance; it should come out into the open, out of the studio. Artists would go about creating their work in the park in full view of the park visitors strolling along. Sometimes the public could even participate in the artist's work. Would I be interested, the following summer, in joining the group of artists that had accepted? I would use food as my medium, and people would watch me create recipes. I would have a morning cooking class for local children, and I would be paid for my work and housed. The programme would last two months. The list of artists was impressive and when they said I could bring Thomas, I readily accepted. I was proud to be included as an artist.

143

The following July, with my six-year-old son Thomas in tow, I drove to Buffalo and then on to Lewiston.

The park was located on the Hudson River, two hundred acres, with a magnificent view of the gorge just beyond the Niagara Falls. Along the pathways of the park were studios for artists, but during that first summer we worked in makeshift studios. I was given a table, a hot plate and nothing else. Nobody had prepared anything, so I went shopping in Buffalo and bought everything I thought I would need for the children's cooking classes. I had read in the *New York Times* about a month before of a man who was importing a new gadget called the "Cuisinart food processor", based on a French restaurant appliance. The electric utensil could mix, cut, shred and beat, and the *New York Times* called it a miracle machine. So I called Cuisinart in Connecticut and suggested that they send me a food processor. In exchange, I would demonstrate the appliance as I prepared food and distribute pamphlets to the crowd. They agreed, and two days later I received my first food processor. I spent an entire day experimenting with the Cuisinart and found it very useful.

In those first few days after my arrival, I went around meeting the artists in residence. There was Catherine Jamlison, a very intense young woman whose medium was photography. She printed her photographs on large white sheets that she spread on the grass so that the rays of the sun could be used like a catalyst. She befriended Thomas who went around for her on his bicycle with a camera strapped to his ankles. Thomas's

144

pictures of grass, insects or paths would be developed to form an artistic pattern on those enormous sheets. Not far from where I was working an artist was building gigantic plastic forms, that looked like enormous Tinkertoys, encouraging the public to join him. I met Charles Simmonds, a sculptor who built cities in holes in walls on the streets of New York. His miniature villages were made of bricks the size of grains of rice. He had a big project at Art Park; he was to build a house made with bags of earth filled with seeds. After rain, the house would sprout, and corn and other vegetables would grow. In the mornings he, like me, was to teach a group of children how to make the tiny bricks he used in his art, so they could build their own cities. As yet, neither he nor I had any children for our classes. I suggested to the manager of Art Park that he should go on the radio and invite children to join us for a free cooking class and an art class. They would start with me, then go on to Charles. It worked, and within days we both had a large group of children. I taught them the basics of cooking and made something they could eat for lunch. We made *omelettes*, *crêpes*, grated carrot salad, sautéd chicken, rhubarb mousse, and many other dishes. While the children tried to cook, Bob Sacha, a young Lewiston photographer, took pictures of them for the park. The food processor was a great help since in the afternoon I often had a hundred people watching me create dishes which they all wanted to taste. In the late afternoon, when the park closed, the artists would meet in one of the buildings. I often cooked for them or brought along dishes I had

145

prepared during the day. One day a week I took off with Thomas. We explored the Niagara Falls, or drove to Canada for dinner. Both Thomas and I had a great time. When we left Art Park, Catherine Jamlison handed me a sheet with pictures of Thomas running around, playing or helping her with her work. I framed the sheet, and to this day it's hanging in our house.

Back in New York, the book *Cooking with Colette* was ready to go to press. The production people asked for a picture of me cooking with the children. I remembered that Bob Sacha had taken many pictures of us, so I asked him for one. He sent a great photo of me looking on as a child tries to separate an egg. I wanted to use the picture for the cover of the book, but we needed consent and Bob Sacha didn't know who the little girl was. Hundreds of children had come to my stand in Art Park. How was I going to find her? Jimmy had a brilliant idea. We'd call the Chief of Police of Lewiston and ask for his help. We sent him the picture. Unfortunately the police chief didn't know who the girl was, but he sent it on to the local newspaper. The caption in the newspaper read, "Who is this Mystery Child?" Within a few days the little girl was found, and we were able to use her photo for the book.

Soon after *Cooking with Colette* was published I received a telephone call from the *New American Library*. The publisher had heard from Cuisinart that I had experimented with their food processor. Could I write a book about food processors, giving an evaluation of the best available, and develop a few recipes? By this time I had switched from teaching at

146

Hofstra University to St Anne's School, a private school in Brooklyn that my own children attended. I was so busy with schoolwork that I asked a journalist friend, Jill Harris Herman, to help. I would test the food processors and take notes, and then she would write the evaluations while I developed recipes. My kitchen began to resemble an appliance store as I got inspired by the food processors and discovered I could create complicated dishes quickly that, in the past, I had hesitated to prepare. Jill went to work, and Jimmy made line drawings of the processors and dishes. Within six months we had a food processor cookbook and guide.

Meanwhile, Jill and I discovered that there were other well-known food writers writing food processor books, and I began to worry about the competition. Ours was called *A Mostly French Food Processor Cookbook*, and in the fall of 1977 it came out with five others on the same subject! I was very scared, but thankfully the reviews were glowing. The *New York Times* called our book "Outstanding . . . adventurous and inspired." We had a bestseller and the book had to go back to press within a month, which took the publisher and I quite by surprise. Jimmy was very happy with my success, and I felt proud of him too. His projects were praised by the architectural critics and the office was now quite busy. The book was ultimately reprinted several times, and sold over 100,000 copies within a year. I was interviewed on radio and television programmes such as *Good Morning America*.

Although I had earned a certain reputation in the food world through my articles, the cooking school and

Cooking with Colette, the success of this book opened new doors for me. My life was no longer the same: I started to meet other food writers and food critics; I was asked to lunches which, to my regret, I could rarely attend as I was still teaching, but my opinions on food and restaurants were being sought by people in the food world. I met Craig Claiborne, the esteemed restaurant critic of the *New York Times*, who liked to come to dinner. He always brought interesting friends. Sometimes I would see one of the dishes I had served him appear in his Saturday column, and once he brought along the stars of the famed TV show *Upstairs, Downstairs*. My children were in awe and hung about on the staircase all during dinner, trying to catch glimpses of their favourite actors. The following Saturday Craig wrote a profile of me, with the recipes for all the dishes I had served at dinner that night. Jimmy loved the notoriety that my books brought to our family.

I also met Pierre Franey, who wrote a weekly column for the *New York Times*, and Gael Greene, then a young food writer for *New York Magazine*. We struck up a friendship, and she would often call me to ask about new restaurants I had found in Chinatown. She was very generous, and would always credit me as her source.

I also began to meet chefs and was often invited to the opening of new restaurants, which Jimmy loved. I met Andre Soltner of Lutece; Barry Wines of the Quilted Giraffe who, like me, loved Japanese and Chinese cuisine; Larry Forgione at River Café, whose

American Cuisine taught me a lot, but it was with Alice Waters and Jeremiah Towers of Chez Panisse that I really identified. Alice believed in home-grown ingredients, fresh and seasonal. She also brought California's attention to miniature vegetables, French string beans, local fish and meats. For me, they related to the way I actually cooked; they were the future of cooking, and they also seemed to relate to what was happening in Europe, especially in France.

Worldwide, the best-known chef at that time was Paul Bocuse of France. Paul Bocuse had trained at Fernand Point's restaurant La Pyramide and owned a three-star restaurant in the outskirts of Lyon at Collonges-au-Mont-d'Or. Bocuse had just published a book in France called *La Cuisine du Marche*, which had revolutionized French cooking, then considered the best in the world. It illustrated the way the new French chefs ran their restaurants, how they went to market every morning and served only what was in season. The classic recipes of yesteryear were made lighter and more innovative. The book also discussed new trends amongst the French chefs, who employed Japanese cooks in their kitchens, and used Chinese techniques and utensils. In the United States, Pantheon had bought the rights to Paul Bocuse's book and was looking for a translator.

I had met Paul Bocuse many years earlier, on one of the food trips I had taken with my stepfather to La Pyramide. When Pantheon suggested me as a translator, Paul remembered our meeting and, knowing my stepfather, agreed that I should translate the book.

It contained 1200 recipes, exhaustive step-by-step instructions on various methods of cooking, and stories about him and his family. This was a monumental job, and I had never tackled anything like it ever before. I was still teaching full time, taking care of my four children and trying to run a very hectic household. It all seemed too daunting, but I decided to take on the project anyway.

The contract offered me two options: I could either get a substantial fee or I could get a small fee with a share in the royalties. I consulted my agent and talked to my friends in the food world. Everyone agreed that this book was going to be a great success, and that its sales would most probably top those of Julia Child who was the reigning queen of the food world at that time. I also learned that the first printing would be over 100,000 copies and that they predicted sales of over a million. I accepted the job and chose to share in the royalties. Working at night, I began to translate the book.

The first twenty pages seemed easy: Paul's style and explanations were clear, and gave the reader tips that only a chef would know. But when I started to translate the recipes, I had the feeling that they were not Paul Bocuse's. Some assistant must have followed him as he cooked, then later adapted the recipes for domestic use. The problem was that whoever had written the recipes did not know how to cook. I was and am a cook who can easily detect, just by reading a recipe, whether or not it will work. Many of Paul's recipes did not seem to work! Although I was denied a budget for testing, I decided to try some of the recipes in my own kitchen anyway. The results were deplorable.

I contacted Pantheon and suggested they send me to Lyon to talk over the recipes with Paul. The answer was a no; but I could telephone him and discuss them that way. I tried several times. Paul was either too busy or away, and would refer me to his assistant who, I was sure, was the one who had written the book. Her response was always the same: *"Non, Madame Rossant, les recettes sont parfaites!"* (No, Mrs Rossant, the recipes are perfect). I stopped calling after I translated the *coq au vin* recipe which called for two litres of red wine for a four pound chicken. I had tested the recipe and found I had a *coq au vin* soup! Her answer to me was the same as usual: the recipe was correct. So I started to change the recipes but always wrote explanations for the changes in the margins.

The book came out in the spring. Paul Bocuse, his wife and his *chefs de cuisine* were put up at the Pierre Hotel. I was to meet Paul and accompany him to interviews and translate for him, as he did not speak a word of English.

On the day of publication Paul was to prepare a dinner at Lutece for the press. We were to meet for the first time in twenty-five years at 7.30 a.m. in front of Balducci's food store on Sixth Avenue to shop for the dinner. Paul had brought many things from France, but we needed meat, vegetables and fruit. I recognized him immediately. Paul was a tall, imposing man with a prominent French nose and a ready smile. He embraced me heartily, nearly breaking all the bones in my back. A few journalists began to assemble and Paul, acting like a great star, spoke with them as I, standing shyly behind him, translated their questions and his answers. Unfortunately, Balducci had forgotten our appointment and the store was not yet open — we were too early.

"Colette, I need breakfast, where shall we go?" I looked around. Nothing was open except McDonald's. I tried to explain that McDonald's, which had not as yet invaded France, was a fast food chain and there wouldn't be much he would like. "Let's go there, it's fine," and so to McDonald's we went, followed by the press. As we sat down, I explained to Paul what was on the menu.

"You can have a muffin with an egg and cheese, or ham."

"Muffin? What is a muffin?"

I explained and Paul chose the muffin with egg and ham and french fries. Paul ate the eggs with gusto, thought the coffee was too weak, but announced loudly: "These are the best french fries I have ever eaten. I want to meet the chef."

"But Paul, this is a fast food restaurant, there is no chef."

"Nonsense Colette, every kitchen has a chef!"

With these words Paul got up and walked over to the counter where a young black man was standing, waiting to receive orders. To his astonishment and amidst the flashes of the photographers, Paul insisted on shaking his hand and saying over and over again *"Bravo, jeune homme. Les meilleures frites que j'ai jamais mangées. Traduisez, Colette."*

There were large headlines that evening in the papers: "Paul Bocuse eats the world's best french fries in New York at McDonald's."

The dinner at Lutece went well and for the next two days we ran around the city. Bocuse appeared on all the talk shows and I, always trailing behind, translated everything he said. He loved American veal . . . believed our beef was the best in the world . . . he liked Californian wines, said their vegetables were great . . . but he missed French salad, bread and butter.

On the Wednesday Pantheon received a call from Julia Child. In two days she would be opening Faneuil Hall Marketplace in Boston with the Mayor. She wanted Paul Bocuse to join her, and then they would both go to her home and together cook dinner for the press. Pantheon was in heaven. Julia Child, the grand dame of American food, was endorsing Paul Bocuse! Paul accepted, and I was told to call Julia Child to make the arrangements. We would both go to Boston and I would continue to translate for him although Julia understood French very well. On Thursday Paul received a call from the Rolex watch company. Would he pose for them the next day for a rather substantial sum of money? Paul accepted and announced that he would forgo the trip to Boston. I pleaded with him, Pantheon pleaded, but Paul would not change his mind. I tried to explain who Julia Child was, how important she was to the American public, what could she do for the success or failure of his book. Nothing would budge him from his decision — he would not go, and that was final!

I was told to call Julia Child and announce the bad news. Julia was furious with him and unfortunately also with me, as the bearer of the news. The next day, when interviewed on television about Faneuil Hall, Julia was asked what she thought of Paul Bocuse's cookbook. She dismissed it with shrug, "Nothing new," she said, "nothing worth talking about."

The book, which had sold 30,000 copies in the first three days, had now slowed down to a trickle. Our only hope was that, with good publicity, the public would forget Julia Child's comments and again buy Paul Bocuse's book. This was not to happen, because six months later an article appeared in *New York Magazine* claiming that Paul Bocuse had never in fact written the book. He had bought the manuscript from the widow of a young, brilliant chef and adapted the recipes for his restaurant. Pantheon sued Flammarion, the French publisher. Bocuse accused us of not translating the foreword which recounted the story of the manuscript. It turned out that the book that Flammarion had given to Pantheon for the translation was the second edition and in that edition there had been no foreword. Paul had not known which edition I had received. Once the story had made the rounds the book virtually stopped selling, and my dream of riches died with it.

The following summer Paul Bocuse, feeling sorry about what had happened, invited Jimmy and me to Lyon. He wrote, "I will send you off to visit all my

154

friends: the Troisgros, Michel Guérard and Louis Outhier. So, come and see me." And so we did.

Bocuse's restaurant was just outside Lyon. Paul received us in full chef's regalia, and we were given the royal treatment. He ordered all the dishes that had made him famous, and that I had translated but never tasted. We enjoyed the signature soup he had made for the French president, Giscard d'Estaing, earning him the title of Meilleur Ouvrier de France. The soup was called *soupe aux truffes Élysée*, a very strongly flavoured chicken *consommé*, with thick slices of black truffle swimming in it. It was sealed with a golden, buttery dome of flaky pastry. You broke the pastry dome and suddenly you were engulfed by the truffle's strong, earthy aroma. This dish was followed by mullet served with a pistou sauce, then partridge with cabbage, and for dessert the most beautiful *croquet-en-bouche*, tiny *pâte à choux* filled with cream and glazed with spun sugar. For the next two days Paul took us around Lyon and talked about his pet project: an Oscar for food. (Three years later, true to his word the Bocuse d'Or was born and I was asked to be a judge for the first event.)

A few days later, going south, we stopped at Roannes at the brothers Troisgros' restaurant. Jean Troisgros was the younger of the two. A handsome man who loved food, tennis and architecture, Jean was in the process of remodelling his kitchen. When he discovered that Jimmy was an architect he kidnapped him and, as they drank 100-year-old Armagnac, discussed the remodelling of his restaurant. While they were both thus occupied, I was told to go and observe how a famous kitchen was run. The kitchen staff put me in a corner near a giant, stainless-steel vat filled with boiling water. I looked around and was astonished by the noise and the speed with which everyone cooked. Then I turned my attention to the vat and wondered what it was for. Soon I understood it was for making the *consommé* used in cooking. Every bone, every leftover raw vegetable went into the vat. The young chefs would throw chicken bones from their cooking stations, like basketball players throwing a ball. They never missed! What made this vat different from the others I had seen before was that it had its own stove and was gargantuan. At the bottom of the vat was a tap. From time to time a young apprentice would come and, after first removing the scum that was building on top and adding salt and freshly ground pepper, would retrieve some broth for the *chef de cuisine*. The broth was then strained, degreased and used for preparing Troisgros famous *filet de boeuf au bouillon de pot-au-feu* (a piece of tender beef poached in this strong delectable *consommé*), which we were served at dinner that night. The meat was so tender one could cut it with a fork.

Once Jimmy had visited the architect in charge of the remodelling of the restaurant and made some suggestions, we left for Saulieu and Bernard Loiseau's La Côte d'Or restaurant with a care package of home-made sausage, fresh bread and a bottle of Troisgros' best wine.

Bernard Loiseau was also young, but less of a star than Bocuse and more of a family man than Jean

Troisgros. In his restaurant we talked about his children and ours, and I felt very much at home with him. We dined on breast of chicken poached with truffles and surrounded with slices of *foie gras*, so rich and tender that I can still taste it. The remainder of the meal is a blur. The next day we drove to Michel Guérard in the Bordeaux region at Les Pres D'Eugenie hotel and restaurant. Michel Guérard, like Paul Bocuse, *was* a star. He was very proud of his hotel and restaurant and felt strongly that he, like Bocuse a few years before, had come up with a new and revolutionary way of cooking. *Cuisine minceur* was his contribution to the new woman, and giving me a meaningful look he said he hoped I would try it. He promised me that his *menu minceur* (a gourmet diet menu) would enable me to shed the few pounds I had acquired in my quest for good food. I had a poached sole in a very light broth with delicate miniature vegetables that simply disappeared in one bite. Dessert was a fruit *soufflé* made with just egg whites. If I could cook like that I certainly *would* go on his diet.

Jimmy opted for the normal restaurant dinner and splurged on rabbit and Guérard's famous *cannelloni* with herbs. I was jealous of Jimmy, who raved about his meal all the way to our next stop.

Before going on to Outhier's restaurant in the South of France, I needed a rest from all this rich food. We drove to Hendaye, a small town on the Atlantic coast, where thirty years earlier Jimmy had proposed in front of an old-fashioned hardware store. To our disappointment it was now a very modern one. A few days later, rested, we continued on our journey.

L'Oasis, Outhier's restaurant, was beautiful. It was near the sea in the small town of La Napoule, near Cannes. This was to be the end of our trip. Outhier was more like Jean Troisgros; he was tall, very handsome and believed himself to be the best cook in France. He was very proud of his three-star Michelin rating, and was one of the first chefs I had met who was truly international, with restaurants in Thailand and India.

That night I told Outhier what we had done and eaten in the last ten days. He then understood that in order to conquer us and show me what a great chef he was, he had to serve us something lovely but simply cooked, because by now I could no longer eat and wished only for plain yogurt! He served us a frothy *consommé*, light as air with tiny morsels of fresh raw scallops. This was followed by the best *bouillabaisse* I had ever tasted. Just before the next dish arrived, to clear out palates, a small pear and brandy sorbet was placed in front of us. The cool sorbet was so refreshing that suddenly I felt rejuvenated and ate the roast squab that followed with enjoyment.

Later, while I was savouring a fresh *fromage blanc* drizzled with local honey and roasted walnuts, Outhier talked about coming to New York to open a new restaurant. He had trained a young chef who would run the restaurant while he remained at L'Oasis. Three years later he opened Lafayette, a restaurant in the Drake Hotel in New York, with his young chef. Jean-Georges Vongerichten, like his mentor, would become both the darling of New York and one of the United States' best known chefs, and he too would open restaurants around the world.

A few days later we were back in New York, and I contemplated all I had seen and learned during those two weeks travelling in France. The chefs I had visited had served us smaller portions than those served in the New York restaurants. Garnishes had changed. Fresh edible flowers were now used, and the plates were very large and often made of glass instead of China. *Soufflés*, salty or sweet, were made with no flour and flavoured oils were drizzled on vegetables. Steaming and poaching now seemed to be the rule. Fresh fava beans, tiny artichokes, shredded leeks, mange touts and sugar snap peas were the vegetables of choice. Desserts had also changed; for the first time I ate an oriental persimmon mousse topped with pomegranate juice in a French restaurant. Gone were the heavy cakes, to be replaced with strange-tasting ginger sorbet or ice cream flavoured with black pepper. Jean-Georges made potato chips with beetroot and served pig's cheek as a main course. Oriental vegetables appeared on menus and sesame seeds seemed to be in every dish.

Slowly my own way of cooking changed. As I was now teaching in Brooklyn, after work I often walked across Brooklyn Bridge into Chinatown to shop there for our evening meal. I discovered that Chinese butchers carried, as I had seen in French open markets, wild ducks, tiny quails, very young chickens and thin slices of beef or pork that one could cook in a few seconds. Vegetables in Chinese grocery stores were always seasonal and very fresh: asparagus were thick and tender; there was tiny *bok choy*, mange tout leaves and sweet potato leaves that were better than the normal supermarket spinach.

Every night I experimented with new recipes. I started to consider every aspect of a dish, its colour, texture, and overall presentation, as well as the star attraction: taste. I began jotting down the recipes I developed, like a stuffed lemon braised with tiny pearl onions, or Brussels sprouts rolled in sesame seeds. Very soon I had a stack of them, and I decided to write a new cookbook. This one would contain my own recipes and would be based on the way we lived. I wanted to write for working parents who, when they came home, were faced with children clamouring for dinner and had no time to spend on long and arduous recipes. I really believed that there was no reason why a working woman or man could not turn the kitchen into a place for high adventure. I knew it could be done.

My book would be called *Colette Rossant's After-Five Gourmet*, as most people left their work at five. I suggested in my book that they shop on their way home, and give themselves two hours to prepare and serve dinner.

Recipes would be classified by ingredients and time. You could prepare hors d'oeuvres in less than fifteen minutes, such as ricotta with herbs on toasted round bread or a mushroom flan. There were recipes for beef, chicken or fish that took thirty minutes to overnight, depending on the time you had on your hands. At that time I was in charge of organizing exchange programmes abroad for our students, and heading the foreign language department at St Anne's; I had ten teachers to look after and many problems to solve; I was running a household and helping my own children with their work. Despite all these responsibilities, I managed to serve dinners every night following the principles of this new book.

The *After-Five Gourmet* came out in the autumn of 1981. While the book did not become a bestseller like the *Food Processor Cookbook*, I believed it was the best cookbook I had ever written. I still believe it today.

For the next three years I continued to write articles about food and restaurant reviews, and I just didn't think I had another cookbook in me. But one morning I received a call from a friend, Francine Moskowitz. Her daughter was getting married, and to my friend's dismay she was marrying into a very Orthodox Jewish family. Although Francine was Jewish, her family was secular and disliked traditional kosher food. Furthermore, most of her daughter's friends were also non-observant.

"Colette, you have to help me. You've got to devise the wedding menu and prepare it in a kosher kitchen in the hall where the wedding will take place."

"Impossible, I can't. I know nothing about kosher cuisine."

"I will give you the name of a rabbi — he will help you and teach you what you can and cannot serve. You can invent new dishes. I know you can do it. Please Colette, don't let me down!"

During the next few weeks I trotted down to the Jewish seminary to talk to the rabbis there about my menu and what I could serve and what I could not. The major challenge for me was that I couldn't use any dairy; I had never cooked without butter or cream.

For a few weeks I worked in the kitchen, buying meat and poultry at kosher butchers. In Chinatown I had discovered a new bean curd, very light, very creamy. So I went back to the seminary to ask if the rabbis thought I could use bean curd. Was it kosher? Could I serve it at a meal that included meat? A few days later I received the answer: Yes, I could replace cream in my recipes with bean curd.

I went back to work, and by the end of the month I had a menu ready which was approved by the bride and her mother. I wrote down the recipes for the catering kitchen and waited anxiously for the wedding day.

The wedding day finally came. After the traditional ceremony, drinks were served accompanied by cherry tomatoes filled with my own version of chopped chicken liver, and mushrooms stuffed with baked salmon and capers. At this point, though, there was too much excitement for anyone to notice the food. Then we all sat down to dinner. Some eyebrows were raised when the appetizer arrived: stuffed smoked salmon with asparagus purée, followed by a veal *pâté* on a bed of endives.

When the main course came along, a shoulder of lamb with Japanese *shiso* leaves served with a julienne of young vegetables and fresh noodles in a mushroom sauce, or fresh whole red snapper stuffed with fennel, I heard murmurs. Just before the dessert, toasts were made by family and friends; then the rabbi who had officiated got up, and after toasting the bride and the groom, called for a round of applause for the cook. "This was the best wedding dinner I have ever had!" said the Rabbi, as he raised his glass to me. Everyone relaxed and joined in. I had succeeded. The wedding dinner had been a strictly kosher meal, and yet it had been elegant, light, very much "nouvelle cuisine". By the time dessert was served, a tower of tiny baked *choux* filled with a raspberry purée and enveloped in a net of spun sugar, dozens of wedding guests were approaching me asking for recipes.

A few days later I received a call from an editor at Arbor House, a small publishing house in Manhattan. "I was a guest at the wedding you catered," he said, "I was very taken by your work and would like to talk to you about doing a kosher cookbook."

When we met he told me that there was a tremendous religious revival taking place across the United States. Many young Jews were tracing their roots and yearning for family, tradition and a sense of belonging, but with added sophistication. The newly observant people knew what good food was; they were *au courant* when it came to eating. Their knowledge of wines was impressive, their taste in food refined, yet they had an unwavering determination to respect Jewish dietary laws, and this is where I came in.

"I want you to write a cookbook expressing the 'new Jewish cuisine'. We're a small company and I can't give you a large advance, but I can pay you for the recipes

163

and give a larger than usual share in the profits. This book will be a great success."

Why did I agree to these terms? I don't know — for the challenge of creating something new? And so I went to work. Every week I sent recipes to the Jewish seminary, to be sure that there would be no mistakes. The book was published in the spring of 1986 and we all waited to see the miracle of everyone rushing to buy it, but this failed to happen. My kosher cookbook was too untraditional, especially in the face of the new revival of Orthodoxy. The press ignored the book, the public didn't buy it and the publisher went bankrupt. Once again I had lost! I swore I would never again write another cookbook.

However the future proved me wrong. Over the next few years, because of my travels and my adventures, I would write three more cookbooks, two memoirs and the book you are reading now.

Roast Quails

Preheat oven to 190°C/375°F/gas mark 5. In a bowl mix together 2 tablespoons soy sauce with 2 tablespoons olive oil and 2 tablespoons grated fresh ginger. Rub 8 quails with the soy mixture. Place 1 kumquat in the cavity of each quail along with a sprig of thyme. Sprinkle with salt and pepper to taste. Place the quails side by side in a baking pan. Add 450ml/16fl oz of chicken stock to the pan and bake the quails for 35 minutes or until they are golden brown. Serves 4.

Poached Salmon with Spinach Tarragon Sauce

Heat 1.5 litres/3 pints of water in a deep skillet. Add 1 carrot sliced, 1 small onion stuck with 2 cloves, 1 bay leaf and 5 peppercorns. Bring to a boil, lower the heat to medium and cook for 10 minutes. Then add 4 salmon steaks. Bring the liquid to a boil, lower the heat to medium and cook for a further 10 minutes. Remove the salmon steak to a platter. Reserve the cooking liquid.

In a blender or food processor place 150g/5oz of fresh tarragon leaves, 300g/10oz of fresh spinach, stems removed, 150g/5oz watercress, stems removed. Add 3 tablespoons olive oil, 1 tablespoon lemon juice and 225ml/8fl oz of the salmon poaching broth. Process until all the ingredients are puréed. Remove to a bowl, add salt and pepper to taste and serve with the salmon steaks. Serves 4.

Honey Cream with Kiwis

Peel 4 kiwis and slice them. In a saucepan heat 100g/3½ oz of honey and add the sliced kiwis. Poach for 5 minutes. Place the kiwis in a bowl with the honey and refrigerate for 20 minutes. In a large bowl whip 900ml/1½ pints of double cream until stiff. In a food processor purée the kiwis with the honey. Then slowly, while stirring, add the puréed kiwis to the cream. Spoon into individual bowls and refrigerate for 2 hours. In a food processor purée 500g/1lb of fresh raspberries with 2 tablespoons sugar. Serve the kiwi cream garnished with mint leaves and the raspberry sauce. Serves 4.

CHAPTER
SIX

The Travels

Travel had become one of my passions. Every winter I would dream of places to go when school was over. I wanted to see the world, and I wanted my children to share my experiences. In fact we travelled mostly with the children; sometimes it was just Jimmy and I.

But now times were difficult. New York in 1975 was in the throes of a serious recession, and Jimmy's office had lost several projects. Marianne was starting her first year in college, Juliette was a senior in high school and applying to colleges, Cecile was a junior and Thomas was about to enter the fifth grade. In a year we would have two children in college and we were both quite worried about the implications of this new financial burden. It would probably mean no trips abroad, and no vacations for the children. Money would be scarce, and the colleges my children were applying to were very expensive. I looked for more freelance work and Jimmy, who hoped to sell some of his drawings, searched for a gallery that would show his work.

The following year Juliette was accepted at Dartmouth, and Marianne transferred to New York University. Our fears were realized; we now had two children in private universities, but fate was on our side and by and by help came in a very unusual way.

One evening two years later, while we were having dinner, Jimmy told me that Habitat, a branch of the UN, was looking for an architect to go to Tanzania to review the design of the planned new capital city, Dodoma. The plan, prepared by a Canadian firm, had pleased no one. The President of Tanzania did not like it and nor did the UN experts who had studied its design. Tanzania? Where was Tanzania? We rushed to an Atlas. Tanzania, Thomas read with awe, was far away in East Africa, near Zanzibar and between Kenya and Uganda. Thomas read that Swahili was the National language, although everyone in school had to learn English, and that Tanzania had a Socialist government with a leader called Julius Nyerere. We all looked at Jimmy. Would he apply for the job? Jimmy looked at me. He saw in my face that I was worried. This was a winter trip, I worked, and the children were in school. "It's only for three months," he said. We had never been separated for more than a week in almost twenty years! Three months! "Of course you must apply," I said, trying to be a good wife, "it sounds so exciting." I was petrified.

In early September 1978 Jimmy left for Tanzania. I heard from him at least once a week.

"Are you happy? How's the work?"

"Difficult. The country is fascinating and very beautiful. There are lots of problems with the Canadians. Food is terrible: English, bland, and very little of it."

"What problems? Are you OK?"

"Can't explain on the phone. I'll write and . . ."

The telephone would go dead. This happened again and again and was very frustrating. On the phone I could never tell Jimmy what was happening at home in New York. He hadn't asked how I was, or about the children, nor did he answer pressing questions, such as the bathroom on the top floor is leaking — what do I do, who do I call?

In late October I received a letter from Jimmy saying that the job was exciting; the plan they were reviewing was, as predicted, not very good; he was drawing a lot; he had befriended some of the Tanzanian planners and was working hard.

A few days later he called:

"Listen, I met the President. We got along; he's a very interesting man. He has grey hair like me. By the way, I don't think I'll be able to be back for Christmas."

"What, what did you say?"

"There's too much work."

And once again the telephone went dead.

Not back for Christmas? Had I heard correctly? I was crushed; Christmas was a very important holiday for me. As a child in Cairo, I always dreamed of spending Christmas with my mother, but it never happened. When Marianne was born I promised myself to always be there for Christmas, to have a tree with lots of presents under it. Up to that day I had kept that promise. But now, without Jimmy, Christmas would not be the same. I was very upset.

Suddenly, a week before Christmas, Jimmy called and asked me to join him. He had a few days off and he would love it if I came. Leave New York and the children? Who would take care of Cecile and Thomas? Could I really go and leave them alone for ten days? Marianne was already home from college for the holidays, so I asked her what she thought and she said, "Don't be ridiculous! I'll be here and there's Lucy. Juliette and I will take care of everything. We can celebrate Christmas a couple of days before, and then you can go."

A few days before Christmas, as soon as school let out, we bought a tree and decorated it. On the evening of the 22nd, I placed all the presents under the tree and we opened them together the next morning. That night, bundled up in my winter clothes and heavy boots, carrying a suitcase filled with summer clothes and food, and after many speeches, hugs and goodbyes to the children and Lucy, I left via London for Tanzania. I arrived in Dar es Salaam on Christmas morning, laden with gifts that Jimmy had requested — tinned *pâtés*, tuna, sardines, packages of cookies and cakes, and a bra for the wife of one of the officials in Dodoma. I had roamed New York City looking for that bra — a size 44 DD!

Dar es Salaam airport seemed primitive; a large wooden structure, open on all sides. Luggage was carried by hand to and from the planes. After going through customs and a passport check, I looked for my luggage and Jimmy. I found neither. Women in brightly coloured wraps and men in khaki safari suits were moving around seemingly without purpose, unaffected by the confusion, the humidity, the noise. In my winter coat and boots, I felt faint from the heat. What should I do if he didn't show up? I knew no one here.

Finally I saw Jimmy running to greet me. "Sorry, sorry . . . I was in a meeting . . . forgot the time," he panted. His embrace soothed me, but I had to tell him the bad news. "No luggage . . . it's lost." Jimmy looked around, found an airline official, and displaying his UN credentials he asked for help. "No problem, Mzee Jim, we will find it soon and bring it to the hotel. No problem!" No Problem was an expression I would hear time and time again in Tanzania.

We were informed that our cookie-cutter hotel, ten stories high with balconies overlooking a boulevard, had no hot water until late afternoon. I needed a shower desperately, but I had to wait, so Jimmy took me for a walk around town. The streets smelled vaguely of gasoline and fried food, but my hunger overcame my slight nausea. Jimmy said that the best food in Dar was Indian. As we sat down in an open-air Indian café, I looked at him. Over the past three months he had changed a lot. In New York he was often tense, nervous and worried. Today he seemed relaxed, joyful and smiling. He looked so comfortable, so at home in this little Indian restaurant. He had lost weight and looked at least ten years younger. I smiled at him, happy to see him so well and as I munched on tiny delicious *samosa*, fried dough filled with spicy meat and potatoes, I listened to his chatter. He explained that a very large Indian population had immigrated to Tanzania when

170

the English were building the East African railroad system. He had many Indian friends in Dodoma. As he ordered the next dish, a highly seasoned chicken curry, more sauce than chicken, and an excellent ice-cold Tanzanian beer bottled in unlabelled brown glass, he told me that the calculators he had asked me to bring were for them. The Indians in Dodoma were Sikhs and mainly worked in the construction business. I learned that trouble was brewing between the Canadian team, who had developed the plan, and the Tanzanians.

"Let's have some dessert, *la specialitée de la maison*," he said mockingly. It was something that I had never seen before, bright orange twirls of dough deep-fried and soaked in honey. More beer please . . . this was pure sugar!

Back at the hotel, no suitcase and no hot water. I removed my boots and my tights, full of ladders, and rinsed my swollen feet in cool water. We were going to have dinner with George Kahama, Director of the CDA (Capital Development Authority) and his wife. What about shoes? Could I at least buy some shoes? Out again, down to the main shopping street. As I looked at the shoe stores, I realized that all the shoes had five- to six-inch heels, most of them platform. I tried several pairs and finally settled on one that didn't seem as high, and out I went, tottering as if I were walking on eggs, but certainly better off than in heavy winter boots. Kahama arrived on time, a small, charming and rotund man with an easy laugh, wearing an elegant safari suit. His wife was twice his size, beautiful, with a regal bearing. I realized then that the bra was for her. She

171

was wearing a long, flowing white dress, and around her shoulders was draped a yellow and green *kinte* cloth with political slogans all over it. The effect was stunning. I told my sad story: no suitcase, no clothes. She smiled and said it would come back to me, "No problem!"

The next morning a package arrived for me at the hotel. Inside was a long, blue dress, much like the one Kahama's wife had worn. A handwritten note said that her dressmaker had made it for me overnight, and that she hoped it would fit me. She hoped I would find my suitcase soon. I am sure I did not look as beautiful in it as she had in hers, but I was thankful for being able to change into clean clothes.

The city's dilapidated houses, the broken sidewalks, the children walking barefoot, and the beggars all disturbed me. But I was in awe of the fish market, sprawling on a sandy beach near the harbour. Thin, shirtless men were calling out to shoppers to view their enormous kingfish, prawns, and sharks. One vendor was cooking prawns in a huge wok-like pan over an open fire. Jimmy walked by my side, at ease with the scene, explaining that President Nyerere, a socialist leader, had transformed the country by making education mandatory, and by regrouping the population into new villages, each built around a central square with a clinic, party headquarters and a school. But the country was still very poor, and corruption in Dar es Salaam, he told me solemnly, was rampant. Nyerere hoped to change this by moving the capital to Dodoma, now a village in the country's interior, which had none of Dar's constant physical reminders of Tanzania's colonial past. Nyerere felt that setting the capital in the centre would help the poorest areas in the country to develop.

Back at the hotel, I called the airline about my suitcase. "No problem," said the man who had answered. "We'll send it on to Dodoma on the next plane." That afternoon we flew to Dodoma.

Dodoma had once been a railway junction between Dar es Salaam and Uganda's capital, Kampala. The Germans had built the railroad and Dodoma, which was then just a small junction town. Much later the English had enlarged the station and built the hotel where we were staying. The hotel was lovely, with low-lying buildings surrounding a magnificent, arcaded courtyard with flowering trees and exotic plants. There were little tables in the shade for afternoon tea and drinks. I felt as if I were part of a Masterpiece Theater series about colonial East Africa.

Jimmy told me what was happening with the new capital plans and his job. Over the past two months, Jimmy had analyzed the plans for the future capital, pointing out all its defects. He had also drawn a preliminary plan of his own which had impressed Kahama, his team of young Tanzanian planners, and even the President. "Now," Jimmy explained, "I have to resign from the job, go back to New York, and re-apply for the job as planner for the city. Then I will be able to bring my own team." What about me? "Well," Jimmy said with excitement in his voice, "you could come with Thomas for three months in the summer and stay here with him in Dodoma. The government would give us a large house with a servant and it would be a marvellous vacation for both of you."

The next day, while Jimmy was in meetings, I roamed around the small town. Low buildings and arcades that housed small shops surrounded Dodoma's main square: a restaurant here and there; a tyre place; a garage, and two Indian grocery stores. I went into one of them; most of the shelves were almost empty, with just a few tins and some vegetables, soap and sprays for cockroaches. Beyond the grocery was a beauty salon. As I looked through the glass I saw women who'd had their hair done in very intricate braids, a fashion that would hit New York years later. Their hair was beautiful; each woman seemed to have a different design. What patience they had!

Next to the beauty salon was an Indian sweet shop offering desserts much like the one I'd had in Dar es Salaam; further down was a small store, a hole in the wall, selling fried *samosa* and other Indian dishes. At one corner of the square was a stand selling tiny pieces of liver on skewers and roasted tiny bananas. I tried a couple of bananas and was quite surprised — they were so sweet and their strong aroma was intoxicating.

Near the centre of town were large villas built by the English after World War 1. They now housed expatriates working on the new capital. A little further from the centre were simple, one-storey stucco houses with red-tiled roofs, inhabited by Tanzanians and Indians who owned businesses. Several villages of the Wagogo — (Dodoma's local tribe, Kahama's people who lived

174

in sunken mud houses — surrounded Dodoma. When I recounted what I had done during the day, Jimmy told me that about ten miles out of town there were also encampments of Masai, a tribe who raised large herds of goats and cows.

The town had a country club, left over from the British colonials, with a swimming pool and tennis courts. Today the club's members were Tanzanians who had come from Dar es Salaam to work on the capital project, and wealthy Indians and expats from Scandinavia, England, France and Germany.

That night we ate in a garden restaurant with an enormous grill. Small, scrawny chickens, marinated for an entire day in lime juice, hot peppers, ginger and cloves, were broiled and served with grilled bananas and beer. I was famished and gobbled the moist, lean chicken flesh. I can say now, without a doubt, that the Tanzanian way of preparing fowl is the best I've ever discovered in all my travels. I was so enchanted by the way they cooked the chicken that later on I used their recipe in one of my cookbooks.

A few days later I flew back to Dar es Salam. Jimmy told me he would resign in a few weeks and fly back to New York to wait for the President and Kahama to apply to the UN for his return. As I boarded the plane to New York, "No problem" were the last words I heard. The suitcase turned up two months later after a wonderful vacation.

Once back in New York, Jimmy waited impatiently for word from the UN. Would he be going back to Dodoma to design the centre of the new capital? Six months went by before he received the hoped-for answer. Jimmy and Thomas were jubilant. Thomas insisted that we all take Swahili lessons before the summer.

For the next three weeks, I saw little of Jimmy. He had to choose a team to go with him, and he worked day and night on the preliminary designs. He selected two young architects: John Diebboll, a soulful, quiet 23-year-old who seemed almost to worship his boss, and Tom Anderson, more experienced than John, and quite ambitious, and a few others as well. They all left at the end of March and I promised that I would follow with Thomas in June. Marianne, home from college, would hold the fort in New York, along with my intrepid Lucy. The end of June arrived very quickly and now it was our turn to suffer a slew of injections and quinine pills. Jimmy's letters were full of requests: bring food (there was very little in Dodoma) like tinned beans, sugar, flour, powdered milk, and spices. Don't forget make-up, lots of it, cheap calculators, utility candles, and over-the-counter medicines. Stop in Paris and buy a bicycle for Thomas, along with fresh butter, cheese, cookies, and crackers. A letter would arrive every week with new requests. I ordered a food processor with a transformer and stocked up on shampoo. At the airport, we looked like refugees leaving New York forever.

The plane from Paris to Dodoma stopped in Ethiopia for a couple of hours. As we left the plane, I was told by an airline official that Thomas and I wouldn't be allowed back on the plane because they needed our seats for a Chinese delegation. I stood there dumbfounded. We would have to stay in Addis Ababa for two to three days until another plane came. Sitting on a hard, plastic airport chair I looked at Thomas, whose lanky legs were drawn up to his chin, patiently waiting. I suddenly had an idea. I whispered to him, "Throw yourself on the floor and start moaning. Say you're very sick and try to throw up." Thomas was so convincing that the manager of the airline, fearing that something terrible would happen to my son, decided to put us back on the plane in first class!

The house in Dodoma was large, with two bedrooms, a living/dining room, and a simple kitchen with an electric range and a refrigerator. The sink had only one tap for cold water. The bathroom was rudimentary, but the house was bright and very breezy. There was a lovely garden with an avocado and a papaya tree. Jimmy had chosen a young Tanzanian in his early twenties to help us with the house. Simon (many Tanzanians have two names, one English and one Swahili) would clean, take care of the garden and help me in any way I wanted. He lived two hours away and walked to our house every morning. I stored the butter and cheeses from Paris, and the bread and vegetables from the Dar market in the refrigerator. On our first night there we took Thomas to the chicken restaurant for dinner. Thomas loved it and decided that Dodoma was a great place to be, until we returned home and found the house in darkness. No more electricity! The butter had already melted in the late afternoon heat; we had to find a cool place for the cheeses and the vegetables. We lit candles and undressed in semi-darkness.

"When will the electricity come back?" I asked. Jimmy smiled. "I don't know. The roads from Dar es Salaam are flooded and the new electric generator is stuck in the harbour. This is a poor country, but don't worry, we'll manage quite well." I lay next to Jimmy on our thin mattress, somewhat incredulous that we were living in this tiny African village. Suddenly, I heard a light thud on our bed, as if something had fallen from the ceiling. I screamed, Jimmy lit a candle and we looked down. On the sheet were two small lizards, light green and about four inches long; six more were still clinging to the ceiling. Jimmy tried to reassure me.

"Don't be afraid . . . relax, Colette . . . they're harmless."

"I hate lizards and large bugs."

"But these are very friendly; in fact, they eat the bugs that would hurt you."

With this statement, he swept our new friends off our blanket.

For the next few weeks, I would count the lizards on the ceiling before I closed my eyes. If they were only a few — three or four — I'd fall asleep, but if there were more, I had a hard time. When finally I admitted to Simon that I was afraid of lizards, he made a point of removing most of them with a broom just before he left the house. I was grateful for this.

For the next three months, electricity came on for a couple of hours a day or not at all. We learned to go to bed at dusk and rise with the sun. We also learned to read by candlelight. We took turns, one reading aloud to the other two. If Lincoln had done it, Thomas reasoned, then why couldn't we?

Preparing meals was another problem, but one that, in retrospect, taught me a great deal about how to be both resilient and creative in my cooking. The electric range was, of course, useless. Simon bought us a small, locally made charcoal stove (a cylinder of tin), and every morning he came from his village with a bag of charcoal and twigs and lit a fire for our breakfast, repeating this indispensable service at lunch and dinner. I tried to replicate his actions several times, but had no luck lighting the stove.

What to cook? Every day Dodoma's central square had a market. Farmers would come from around Dodoma, but there was very little to buy. Vendors squatted on the dusty ground in front of their produce: a few piles of aubergines (three to a pile); tomatoes, again three to a pile; tiny, sweet mangoes; cherimoyas; dried fish (infested with flies) from the river. Then there were mountains of *ugali*, the maize that Tanzanians cook like polenta; and also tiny potatoes, which turned out to be delicious. What I needed most was oil, butter, and especially bread. There was one baker in town, a Greek who had lived in Dodoma for forty years. Every day, as I entered the store, he would say, "None today. Tomorrow there'll be bread. No problem." We went days at a time without bread.

Chickens were small and sold live. If I wanted one, I had to kill it myself. One day I gave in, bought a chicken, and took it home, holding the squirming bird by its feet. I went out to the back yard, called Thomas for moral support, and cut its neck with my one sharp knife by holding its body between my knees. I screamed like a wounded animal as I did the deed. Then I had to eviscerate it! All my years of cooking hadn't prepared me for this. How do you pluck a chicken without pulling off all the skin with the feathers? I should have brought the *Joy of Cooking* with me; it would have helped, I'm sure. I felt like a pioneer's wife who had not married into her own class. And I rather enjoyed the disgusting romance of it!

That night we ate dry, skinless, grilled chicken, but it was better than another can of sardines. We hadn't had meat in almost a week. There *was* a butcher on the square, of course. But his chunks — I wondered if he'd *torn* them off — of goat and beef were plagued with buzzing flies and hung drearily in rows on metal hooks. When I asked for a pound, I got half a pound of meat along with another half pound of fat, gristle and bone. An expatriate neighbour, a bird-like English woman, advised me that if I cooked the meat until it was overdone, the flies didn't matter. But I just could not persuade myself to buy it again.

For the next few days we survived on eggs, but our life changed when I was told about the Saturday Market. It was located near the slaughterhouse on a dusty plain near a small creek outside Dodoma, and it was where the Masai brought their lambs, goats and calves to be slaughtered. Crouching in the dirt were women selling brilliantly coloured cloth that they would wear wrapped around their bodies, sometimes even over cotton, American-style dresses. There were stands for wooden bowls; dark, glossy shepherds' clubs carved from single branches of a tree; enamelled cooking utensils; flat leather thongs. But the Saturday Market was mainly for live and butchered goats, sheep and cattle from the slaughterhouse.

The very first Saturday I visited the market, I made an ally in Philip, a short, wiry young butcher who sold small goats from a wooden stand. For a few minutes I watched him cutting up goats with a machete-like knife, like the butchers at the daily market in Dodoma's central square. Suddenly I had an idea. I proposed a plan that would benefit us both: I'd teach him how to butcher goats in the European way, and he would gain expatriate clients willing to pay a much higher price for the meat. Philip agreed and told me to meet him the next day. As I drove our dusty white Peugeot station wagon (a vehicle ubiquitous in East Africa) to the slaughterhouse, I hoped that I really knew how to carve a goat. After all, I was French and remembered the proper French cuts of lamb and beef. Furthermore, I had often cut up chickens or deboned a duck. I also remembered the diagram of a cow with the different pieces of meat so well-defined in Fanny Farmer's cookbook. Could butchering a goat be so very different?

To the rear of Philip's stand, I found a whole goat splayed on the table. Philip handed me a machete with a long, curved, menacing blade. I told Philip that I would guide him, but that he would have to do the cutting himself. The lessons began.

"First," I said, "cut the goat in half lengthwise, following the backbone." This exposed the liver, which I pulled out warm, my hand shaking. I then told him to remove the entrails. Trying not to feel too sick, I turned away while he did that. I looked for the kidneys and wasn't very sure where they were, but once he'd removed the entrails I saw them. I knew that the European expatriates, especially the British, would love them, and I told Philip that. Then I carefully showed him how to carve the leg (it would be delicious broiled), and the small chops from the upper ribs. I was speaking to him as if in a trance, allowing instinct to guide me. Philip too seemed to transform himself almost spiritually into a butcher-artist. He went at the shoulder with intense focus, while he listened to my directions to cut the meat into even cubes for stew, and showed professional pleasure as he carved out the small, tender-looking fillet. We cut up two goats that day. As I left, I reminded him to keep the fillet and the liver for me, and I promised to buy them each Saturday. I also promised that if he butchered the goat the new way from now on, I would tell all the expatriates in town to buy exclusively from him.

Back home, I marinated the fillet in lime juice and thyme and local pepper and broiled it on our charcoal stove. We ate tender roast goat with small potatoes. It was the best dinner we had had at home in weeks. The next day I invited Jimmy's team to dinner and, after marinating the liver in vinegar, lime juice and a small green leaf that tasted like lemon that I found in the market (to this day I don't know what it was), I broiled it and served it with onions and tomatoes.

The next day, as I had promised Philip, I went visiting. Obliged to drink endless cups of tea and nibble on stale biscuits after I knocked on each expatriate's door, I managed to notify most of our neighbourhood about Philip's specially butchered meat. The following Saturday, I arrived at the market and saw a line of people waiting to be served at Philip's stall. When he saw me smiling, he winked and handed me a package. "For you," he said. "No money . . . every week, come."

My next task was to solve the bread problem. I thought I could make bread myself, but I had no oven. Could I make pita on hot stones like I had seen Arabs do it in Egyptian villages? But I had no recipe for Arab bread. A few days later I met a young Swiss engineer who was in Dodoma teaching Tanzanians how to use solar power for cooking instead of charcoal. Tanzania's forests had been decimated over the years, and a reforestation effort had begun. But Tanzanians were so used to cooking with charcoal, and the health of these sparse forests was still being threatened. When I mentioned that I was trying to bake bread, he offered to make me a solar oven. A few days later he came over with what looked like a long tube of metal lined with foil and topped with a piece of glass. All I had to do, he explained, was to place the bread on the foil, close the glass oven door, and stick the whole contraption in the sun. Great, I thought, but I didn't have any idea how to make the dough! A couple who lived next door had once lived in the Australian outback. I decided to ask the wife, Mary — a suntanned, lined woman of fifty — for a recipe. She complied, and threw in a couple of packets of yeast along with a well-worn paperback cookbook detailing the basics of Australian-style bread. Once I'd mixed all the ingredients, Thomas kneaded it with a vengeance. It not only rose, but nearly exploded out of my wooden bowl. We shaped the dough into two baguettes, stuck them in the tubular oven, and perched it on a flat rock in the sun. Thomas squatted right by it and waited, staring through the glass. It took two hours for those loaves to bake, and they came out dense and a bit chewy, but we had succeeded nonetheless.

From that day on, we baked bread once a week. We played around with the recipe and the loaves improved over time — but only slightly.

Every morning Thomas and I took a walk through the town, going from store to store, trying to find things to cook. Indian Sikhs owned most of the shops, and also ran construction companies and exchanged currency with the expatriate community. These shops were invariably dimly lit and sparsely stocked. You might find aspirin, Pepto-Bismol, make-up, toilet paper, potatoes and the Tanzanian staple, *ugali* flour. One day, as we entered one of the stores (whose owner Jimmy knew quite well), I saw a woman leaving with a basket filled with vegetables. I asked the young Indian woman wearing a summer sari who always stood patiently behind the counter if I, too, could have some fresh vegetables. Selma paused and looked at me with curiosity. "Do you have any make-up to sell?" she asked in a whisper. I remembered all the make-up I had bought in New York. "Yes," I said, "I do." She asked me to bring it to her the next day, assuring me that she'd sell me some vegetables.

That night, after I told Jimmy about my encounter, he told me that the Sikhs ran a clandestine bus from Dodoma over into Kenya, because Nyerere had officially closed the border between Tanzania and Kenya. (Tanzania had magnificent game parks, but most tourists went to Kenya, which had a more sophisticated tourist industry. But the Kenyans had been bringing the tourists across the border to access Tanzanian parks, and then pocketing the fees.) This bus was a great moneymaking scheme for the Sikhs, who sold the vegetables they brought back from Kenya at a premium price or in exchange for things the young Indian women could not get in Dodoma. The next day I brought the list of vegetables I wanted, along with a large selection of American drugstore eye make-up and one of my larger baskets. Selma told me to come back in two days to collect my vegetables.

Two days later, Selma handed me my basket. It contained vegetables I hadn't asked for, but which I was content with: a cauliflower, overgrown zucchini, and a large head of lettuce. We hadn't had a green salad in nearly a month! Every week from then on I went back to Selma with eye make-up, blushers and creams in exchange for more produce. I later befriended her, and often went to the store for a chat. She had wanted to be a teacher, but here in Dodoma her life was very restricted and the only thing she could do was study by correspondence, which took a long time. "I will have to get married soon," she said. "I am twenty and my father will find me a husband, and I will not be able to continue to study." Sikh women went to temple in groups and, once married, met at one another's houses. I was the first friend Selma had had who was not a Sikh.

A few weeks later, Selma told me that her cousin was getting married; she wondered if I could make something for a dinner her parents were having for the fiancé's family . . . something French, she mused. I thought about the liver Philip was giving me every week; maybe I could make a liver *pâté*. It turned out she had a large charcoal oven at home, so I prepared the ingredients for the *pâté*, assembled it, and took it to her house. We placed it the oven and prayed for the best. Forty minutes later, the *pâté* looked as if I had cooked it in my own oven in New York. It was a great success at the pre-wedding dinner, and I was in business. I made two to three *pâtés* a week in exchange for vegetables and fruit. Bartering had become my way of life.

I made very few friends among the expatriates who let it be known that they didn't quite approve of my friendships with Tanzanians and Sikhs. They tended to avoid me because I often talked about my new Tanzanian friends and their children. There were a few exceptions, including a couple from Holland who had lived in Dodoma for many years. Margaret was an excellent cook and gardener who produced strawberries, spinach, string beans and radishes, and had the best papaya trees in Dodoma. They also had a wonderful garden of local plants, and had parrots and a small monkey. Thomas and I would often visit them for afternoon tea. I think Thomas had a crush on their daughter, Elisabeth, and I loved Margaret's pancakes. Small, thin and round, they were a cross between a *crêpe* and an American pancake.

She served them with stewed strawberries from her garden, and Thomas and I would wolf down at least six at each sitting. She also taught me to have no fear of garden snakes; we had several in our own garden. Her husband Gustaf worked for the government. He was a geologist, and was teaching the Tanzanians to find and mine Tanzanite, a sparkling, diamond-like stone that, when heated, turns a magnificent purple.

Another couple I befriended was Jimmy's Habitat boss and his wife. Mr and Mrs Kidhane Alemayehu were Ethiopian, and had also lived in Dodoma for several years. Mrs Alemayehu came to visit often, dressed in pale-coloured gowns with flowing scarves around her shoulders. She cooked well, serving us spicy chopped beef in a red-hot sauce and vegetables in a green, spicy sauce with *injira*, flat, soft, pancake-like bread prepared with fermented flour. Her table was always beautifully laid out with exotic flowers and silver cutlery. She also prepared some French dishes; she loved hard-boiled eggs in aspic or served with a mayonnaise, or French grated carrot salad. We sat on low stools and ate with our hands, using the bread to pick up the meat or the sauce. I often wondered where she got these wonderful ingredients, but her husband was Jimmy's boss and I never dared ask. Often when she visited me she would sit and question me about America, New York and about French food.

Among the expatriates were Italians, Danes and a large colony of Chinese who ran the local hospital. They would nod when I saw them in town, but they never spoke to us. I would meet one of them soon enough, when I was bitten on my heel by an insect. It hurt a lot and quite soon my heel became so swollen that I knew I had to remove the sting. Thomas and I drove to the Chinese hospital, a white-washed building with benches all around the entrance, teeming with Tanzanians who had some ailment or other, often malaria or the flu, although much later we learned the flu was probably Aids, the epidemic that would soon ravage Tanzania and most of the rest of the continent.

Because we were foreigners, we were immediately taken to the Chinese doctor. I explained what had happened as I looked around the dirty, fly-infested office. Would I lose my foot from the sting or would I lose it from an infection because of the dirt around me? The doctor seemed to read my mind and said, "Go home, open the wound with a clean, sharp knife, and remove the sting. Wash it with alcohol and take these pills. Antibiotics."

When we got home, I burned the blade of a Swiss Army knife and looked at Thomas. Could I really ask Thomas to cut my heel open? Thomas was only twelve, but in the last few months our relationship had changed. He was today as much a friend as a son. I had taken him everywhere with me, as he spoke Swahili better that I did and could converse with people. I discussed my plans with him and often asked his advice. At night, as we could not leave him alone in the house, he came with us as we socialized. And when we read to one another, the books were those he wanted to read. Thomas started to discuss books with us, which he had never done before.

I looked into his large blue-grey eyes and asked, "Can you cut my heel and remove the sting?" Thomas seemed quite confident that he could perform the operation. We poured alcohol on the wound, cut the skin, removed the sting, applied antibiotic ointment, a bandage, and hoped for the best. A few days later my wound had healed.

Another month went by, and a routine set in. Jimmy left the house very early in the morning and came home for lunch, then would return to the office while Thomas and I explored our surroundings. Jimmy would be back by five, often with his team. In New York there had been an almost total separation between Jimmy's office and home. Here in Dodoma, drawings of the new capital were pinned to the wall and often his associates, tired of eating badly, would come and share our dinner. They discussed the plans or the problems they had with the authorities. Thomas listened and sometimes contributed to the talk, because he now knew the city quite well. He had quite a number of Tanzanian friends who often invited him to their houses, so he was aware of how they lived.

In the afternoon, while Thomas was away with his friends, I had nothing much to do, so one day I decided that I would write a new cookbook with recipes that I had dreamed up while cooking with whatever I had found in the market. Most of all I wanted to write a diet book, because Jimmy and Thomas had lost weight but I hadn't. I had stopped smoking and was wolfing down roasted peanuts all day long.

On a large piece of translucent yellow drafting paper, I wrote a list of the vegetables that were available in the Dodoma market, then a list of meats, and another of the seafood I had found. I began to mix and match new, simple recipes and wrote them down with an old typewriter I borrowed from Kahama's office. Very soon I had a long list of recipes, but had to wait until I went back to New York before I was able to test them. (A year later, *Colette's Slim Cuisine* came out. The book was illustrated with Jimmy's drawings of city scenes made out of vegetables, meat, fish and pasta. The press was cool towards the book, and the public too. Could you really lose weight with such scrumptious recipes? read one of the reviews in the newspaper. One could — I was the living proof — but judging by sales, few believed me.)

August was approaching and so was Jimmy's birthday. What could Thomas and I give him? There was really little to buy in Dodoma and the roads to Dar es Salaam were flooded. On one of our walking expeditions, we discovered a local stadium where the Tanzanians played soccer. All around the stadium were small ivory shops selling creamy-white ivory bracelets, necklaces, and rings which were laid out on black cloth. I asked one of the merchants if he could make a piece of ivory jewellery if I gave him a design. "No problem,"

190

he said. I wasn't convinced, but I decided to take the risk. I asked John Diebboll, Jimmy's young assistant, to secretly give me a sketch of the plan of the new capital city, and I asked the ivory dealer to carve the design onto a piece of ivory. "No problem! Come in three days; it will be ready." He told me it would cost me a hundred shillings. I took out my little calculator to see how much this was in dollars. As the man saw it he said, "Nothing! You give me the calculator, and I give you the carving." An incredible deal! My bartering was at its peak.

On the day of Jimmy's birthday, I invited his team and a few of our friends. I handed Jimmy the carving, wrapped up just as the carver had given it to me in a piece of rough black cloth. I was as surprised as Jimmy when he opened it: a large, concave piece of ivory was carved on one side with a perfect outline of the future centre of the capital. He had tears in his eyes when he said, "it's the best birthday gift I ever got!"

Sometimes Jimmy would give me the keys to his jeep. Thomas and I would drive from Dodoma into the bush, visiting small Wagogo villages or Masai encampments. The Masai were very tall and thin, always wrapped in magnificent coloured cloths with intricate bead jewellery around their necks and long, heavy earrings that elongated their ears. The women were also bejewelled but their necklaces were larger, with more intricate designs. They often had a sleeping baby strapped to their back. It was very hard to communicate with them since most spoke a special dialect. The Gogos, on the contrary, spoke Swahili.

Their houses were very strange: rectangular, built of mud and straw, but half sunk into the ground, with extremely low ceilings. Dried gourds, used as drinking vessels, and cooking pots hung from the wooden-pole rafters. Often the gourds would be decorated and sold at the market. The houses were almost bare: a few low stools, a couple of hammocks and, in one corner, a circle of large stones — the stove. The Gogos, although very poor, always greeted us with warmth and offered to share with us whatever drink they had. Their land was barren and difficult to cultivate; there was no industry, no work.

Thomas and I got to know one Wagogo family quite well, and between the family's broken English and our few words of Swahili we managed to learn a lot from them. Their older son went to school; his younger brother could not because he had no shoes, and the school would not admit him without them. The next day we brought along Thomas' old sneakers for the young Wagogo boy. Later we visited the school and were appalled. Housed in a crumbling, white-washed concrete block building around a small courtyard, the school had very few books, and hardly any paper or pencils.

When I went back to New York in the autumn, I asked my friends for donations and sent books, boxes of pencils and shoes to Dodoma, hoping that all the kids in the Wagogo village would be able to go to school.

The following year we returned in the summer to Dodoma. This time I was really prepared, and I knew exactly what food to bring: boxes of flour ready to be turned into bread by just adding water; tins of meats, tins of vegetables, and bras of all sizes for bartering plus clothing for the young Wagogo children and notebooks for the school that I bought in Paris. As this was to be our last summer in Tanzania, Jimmy decided to take us for a long weekend to visit a game park. We flew to the Ngorogoro Crater and saw elephants roaming freely, hippopotamuses swimming and hyenas eating as we waited to drive on. On another weekend, Jimmy and Thomas climbed to the top of Tanzania's highest mountain, Kilimanjaro, while I contented myself with climbing with great difficulty to the first stage.

At the end of the summer, the day before we left Dodoma, a stream of Tanzanians came to bid us good-bye. Our new Wagogo friends came too, carrying dark brown wooden stools made of a single piece of wood, carved ivory bracelets, and multicoloured cloths. For Thomas they brought a ceremonial wooden spear.

To this day I miss Tanzania. I was bitten by the African bug. I loved the country and its people. I had made many friends and, from afar, followed their lives, hoping that one day I would return.

In September 1980, back in New York for the beginning of the school year, I was restless. Once again, I found myself scheming to travel to some faraway country. This time I put all my efforts into finding a way to go to Japan. Japanese restaurants were opening everywhere in New York, and I wanted to learn more about their cuisine.

At my friend Arakawa's suggestion, I joined the Japan Society and met Peter Grilli who was their cultural and movie director. Peter was short and woolly, like a lovable teddy bear. He had been brought up in Japan where his father was a well-known music critic, and he loved Japanese culture and cuisine. He very quickly understood my curiosity for Japanese ingredients and ways of preparing food as I often dragged him to Japanese restaurants asking hundreds of questions. Very quickly I learned that Japanese food wasn't merely *sushi* and *sashimi*, which had started to sweep New York City, but was an incredibly complex and fascinating cuisine. Peter taught me how to order and ask for dishes that were not on the menu, such as soba buckwheat noodles, eaten cold with a dipping sauce, tiny broiled sardines or sautéd aubergine topped with bonito shavings which seemed to be alive, moving in the air.

One day Peter announced that he was organizing a gastronomic tour of Japan for the Japan Society's most important supporters and trustees. I was envious, but the trip was very expensive and I simply could not afford it. A month before they were due to leave, Peter approached me. Would I like to join the group? He needed someone who had some knowledge of Japanese food, someone who would ask intelligent questions and discuss the food with the chefs who were going to prepare very special meals. We would be travelling in Japan for two weeks. The only thing I had to do was to make a small contribution to the Japan Society. The trip was in June so I would be finished with teaching. But what about my four children? I was hoping that Jimmy would be happy for me to go and take care of the younger kids, but it was my friend Elisabeth, once again, who came to the rescue. The children could come and join her family in East Hampton, and Lucy would go with them. Jimmy very reluctantly gave his consent:

"I'll miss you, but I left you when I went to Tanzania," he said with a sad smile, "so now it's your turn, and two weeks is not that long."

On the plane to Tokyo I learned that most of my companions were really going to Japan to buy antiques. No one, it seemed, was too excited about the gastronomic tour, and I understood why Peter had asked me to join them.

On our first evening, Peter announced that we had been invited by the Emperor's principal chef for a *kaiseki* dinner. A *kaiseki* dinner, Peter explained, is based on seasonal food, and also on the chef's mood and inspiration. The dinner proceeds through a series of small dishes, each one a work of art as the dish itself is an important part of the presentation. There is harmony in the order of the dishes, their colour, texture and taste. Just before dinner, he added, the Emperor's chef will demonstrate how he prepares a fish, which will later be served to us as *tempura*.

That night we sat on brocade cushions in a large *tatami* room in a low building attached to the Emperor's palace. In front of us was a low stage with a dark lacquer table where, I assumed, the chef would prepare the fish. When the chef entered the room there was a murmur of astonishment from all of us; he looked like a priest or a great lord from one of Kurasawa's epic films. He wore a black, shiny silk hat tied around his chin, a white, billowing robe with a magnificent gold-thread rope around his waist. As he crouched before the table set in the centre of the stage, two young servants, dressed in black, brought in a silver platter with a large black fish on a bed of seaweed. The chef picked up a long silver chopstick with one hand and a long thin knife with the other and proceeded to fillet the fish, never touching it with his hands. I looked at the chef mesmerized, in awe of his dexterity. How did he do it? The knife seemed to fly from one side of the fish to the other. Like magic, within ten minutes four clean fillets were laid onto the silver platter.

Later we were led to a dining room. There, a low table was laid with twenty black lacquered trays decorated with gold bamboo leaves. Thin slices of a very pale tuna were arranged in the shape of a flower. Near the fish was a small, green glass bowl filled with soy sauce. As we sat down on silk damask cushions, we were offered small *sake* cups, each different, each more beautiful than the next. I choose a pale, white translucent china cup. Into the cups was poured very dry *sake* by beautiful kimono-clad young women.

Slowly the dinner unfolded, one dish after another, each more exquisite than the last. One dish that I will never forget was the *tempura* fish. Our black trays were removed, replaced by pure white translucent trays reminiscent of the chef's white robe. On each tray was a square of bamboo in the shape of the table on which

196

the fish had been cut. The bamboo was surrounded with fresh bamboo leaves. Fish fillets of golden *tempura* were strung on carved wooden skewers and set on top of the leaves. Beside each was a snowy-white mountain of finely grated white radish. A black lacquered bowl with half a gold moon painted on its side was filled with a transparent dipping sauce. It was so amazingly beautiful that I hesitated for a moment to pick up the tiny morsels of fried fish which were crunchy, light, and not at all oily.

Twelve small dishes followed, each intricately prepared, each in its own setting. For dessert we were served a pink-tinted ball on an ice-carved plate. Called cherry blossom *mochi*, it was a sweet, glutinous rice ball stuffed with a red-bean paste and rolled in edible brined cherry leaves. This strange combination of bland soft rice and overly sweet bean, but with a lemony aftertaste, was the perfect finale to a spectacular meal.

The next day we drove about two hours south of Tokyo to a *ryokan*, a traditional Japanese inn, set on the edge of the sea. That night Peter explained to me that near the ocean at the bottom of the hill was a superb *onsen*, a Japanese bath overlooking the sea. If I went very early, say five o'clock in the morning, he explained, I would be alone, and the experience of a Japanese bath was worth getting up at the crack of dawn for. So the next morning, dressed in my kimono and flip-flop slippers, I went down three flights of wooden stairs to the building that housed the bath. A very old man greeted me at the door, and with gestures explained that I should undress and place my clothes in the basket he was handing me. I did as he requested, feeling a bit embarrassed to be naked in front of this old man, but he did not seem to look or care. He then led me to a room surrounded with glass walls. In the centre was a very large pool of hot, clean water. Along the walls were taps and low wooden stools. The old man gestured towards the taps. I understood that I had to wash myself first and rinse the soap off, and then get into the water. I washed, and then slowly slid into the very hot water.

As I stood crouching in the water I looked at the sun slowly rising over the horizon. Its golden rays were playing with the calm surface of the water. I was lost in my dreams. I felt so in tune with my surroundings that I began to think that perhaps in one of my former lives I had been a Japanese noblewoman. The hot water was so relaxing, my surroundings so extraordinary that I forgot the time. Suddenly I realized that I was no longer alone in the pool. As I glanced discreetly behind me I saw four men looking my way. In panic I wondered what should I do? Should I get up, climb the few steps and cross the length of the pool naked? I decided against it and felt that I could wait. These men would not be here for ever. When they left I would get up.

Half an hour went by. The skin of my hands was all crinkled by the heat and water, and the men were still there. I knew I couldn't stay in the water any longer so I decided to get up, climb the steps, and walk across the length of the pool, reasoning that I did not know these men and probably wouldn't see them again. So without looking I did just that, feeling their eyes on me as I went back to the old man to pick up my clothes. At breakfast that morning I told Peter the story just as the same four men entered the dining room and were introduced to us as the owners of the *ryokan*. The men smiled but said nothing, and I looked the other way as Peter laughed at my embarrassment, whispering that I had made their day and he was sure I would be sent flowers. To my total embarrassment, that's exactly what they did!

For the next two weeks we travelled through Japan. We went north to the temple of Issey and there had dinner in the head priest's private dining room, feasting on food I had never eaten before while overlooking a most extraordinary Zen garden of sand and rocks — so incredibly peaceful. Then we went on to a Buddhist temple where we were served a vegetarian dinner that defied the imagination: what we thought was steak was mushrooms; what we thought was fish was vegetables.

Our next stop was Osaka, to visit the famous French-Japanese cooking school and visit the Bunraku Theatre. Later we flew to Kanazawa, on the west coast of Japan. Kanazawa was and is the centre of lacquer and we went to visit a very great lacquer artist, one of the "living treasures" of Japan. Visiting his house was like going to the inner sanctum of a lacquer museum. There was intricately designed furniture, vases, bowls, geisha combs of all sizes. As we left, we each were handed a small box concealing a lovely black and gold lacquer bowl.

The next day we left for Wajima, a small fishing village at the end of a peninsula. It was home to hundreds of types of seaweed, drying in the sun. All along the harbour where the fishermen brought their catch, and the divers their seaweed, was an extraordinary, mile-long vegetable, fish and seaweed market. The women in Wajima, I was told, ran the market. There were stands of long strings of dull-looking seaweed next to piles of shimmering seaweed that I remembered eating in salads. But it was the fish that attracted my attention. There were so many different kinds of fish that I had never seen before: small and large sardines; mountains of miniscule fish that, once dried, would be served on top of rice; there was what looked to me like a young tuna, and near it, whale blubber, a great delicacy for the Japanese. After the fish market, the vegetable stands followed with every colour and shape of aubergine, vats of *miso* filled with cucumbers, carrots and beans that ended up on our table as pickles.

A few days later we flew to Nara to be the guests of the Shogun who offered us dinner in his ancestral home. In a long, pale-green room with sliding *shoji* screens framed in blond wood there were twenty small tables. On the wall was a magnificent calligraphy by a twelfth-century artist, and in a corner, a large pale-blue iris in a slender bamboo vase with silver filigree stood majestically alone. Across the room, two musicians played on ancient violins. As we sat down on low stools, young waitresses brought out dishes, sliding gracefully to the melancholic music of the musicians. The dinner was like a dream.

Our next stop was Kyoto. I loved Kyoto with its temples and gardens, but most of all I loved the indoor market. The market was a mile long, winding around city blocks, selling everything from Kyoto's famed vegetable pickles and the best bean curd I had ever had — transparent, light as air — to embroidered silk kimonos and splendid lacquerware. While my companions were roaming the antiques stores of Kyoto, I spent every minute in the market. On the Sunday I sped to a temple garden where the best flea market in Kyoto was held. I learned to bargain and bought what is today my most precious possession: an iron tea kettle from the eighteenth-century.

I often called home and talked to Jimmy and the children. Jimmy was complaining: he was lonely, and the children missed me. When was I coming back? Soon, I said, wishing that I could continue to travel and explore Japan. But we had already been travelling for two weeks. After Kyoto we were flying back to Tokyo and, to my chagrin, the trip would then be over.

I had a friend in Tokyo. Andre J. was the cultural attaché at the French embassy. A well-known writer, he had been sent to represent French artists in Japan. I had written to him to say that I was coming to Japan and he invited me to stay with him and his wife until the date of my departure. Upon our arrival in Tokyo, I was met at the hotel by Andre's housekeeper, Eufemia, a young Filipino woman. She was to take me to Andre's home, and on the way she told me the most astonishing news: Andre's wife had run away with the Greek cultural attaché! It was a terrible scandal in Tokyo; Andre was crushed, and the French ambassador was embarrassed by the situation. As Eufemia said, it was a mess.

What am I doing here? I asked myself. But my ticket home was not for another three days. I knew no one in Tokyo and Peter had already left for New York. I had no choice but to stay with Andre.

That night, a devasted Andre told me the story and begged me to stay until the end of the month. As cultural attaché, he had to entertain distinguished guests. He needed me. "Please stay, Colette," he said, with tears in his eyes, "I'll pay for your ticket back to New York. I need you." How could I say no? I called Jimmy and begged forgiveness. I had to stay two more weeks in Japan to help Andre cope with the situation. Jimmy was crushed and argued with me for at least ten minutes, and then with a sigh he gave in, saying, "No more than two weeks."

The next day, when Andre had left for the Embassy, I sat down with Eufemia and studied Andre's calendar. He had five dinner parties scheduled for the next two weeks. I asked Eufemia, "What about the menus?"

The cook was also a Filipino. When I studied the menus I thought they were boring, and not festive enough. In these special circumstances we had to offer our guests more exciting fare. Eufemia, who was a very bright, lovely young woman, suggested that she and I go food shopping. She spoke Japanese, and so together we went to the wholesale fish market where I bought tiny little crabs the size of a quarter, and cod fish liver that I would sauté like *foie gras* and serve on a bed of greens. At the vegetable market I bought burdock that looked like French salsify, fresh *shiitake* mushrooms, and Japanese chestnuts to make a mousse for dessert.

The cook and I prepared the first dinner. We sautéd the crabs and served them as appetizers with the drinks, then the cook made a clear soup, adding at the last minute some seaweed I had brought from Wajima. As a main course, I stuffed thin slices of chicken breast with fresh *shiitake* mushrooms and sliced garlic, and surrounded it with a sauce made with the Japanese *uzu* lemon. Tiny potatoes sautéd with rosemary finished the dish. The dessert was a mousse of Japanese persimmons. The dinner was a success and Andre seemed to be calmer.

A few days later Andre told me that among our next guests would be the owners of Seibu, the largest department store in Tokyo which had a very important art museum attached to it. Andre had been planning a major show of French painters and was afraid that Seibu's owners might cancel it. I promised I would make a very special dinner.

On my walks through the Tokyo vegetable market, I had discovered that Japanese cucumbers were very long and narrow, and had very few seeds. I decided that the appetizer would be small chunks of cucumber like miniature wells, filled with salmon caviar entwined with edible greens and topped with *crème fraîche*. They were to be set on *shiso* leaves, and surrounded with vegetable pickles from Kyoto in light aspic. The next course was to be a soup of *azuki* beans with endives, followed by a poached fresh salmon served with pomegranate and *nashi*, a Japanese pear-apple which is today common in the United States but at the time I had never eaten it before. With it I served grated mountain potato mixed with thinly sliced cooked okra and a parsley sauce. For dessert I tried something that I was terrified would not work, a mousse of fresh bean curd with imported raspberries.

That night the owner of Seibu arrived dressed in traditional ancient Japanese clothes, the most beautiful kimono I had ever seen made of silk and silver threads. He was followed by his slender, pale, stunning Japanese wife dressed also in a brocaded kimono of two tones of gold and silver threads. The dinner went very well. Our Seibu guests smiled and complimented me on the dinner. By making a slightly strange dinner, I was afraid that I had ruined Andre's chance of a show at the museum.

The next day I received an invitation from a large publishing house, Kodansha International. To my astonishment, they wanted to talk to me about a cookbook. At the meeting it transpired that our guests of the previous evening had raved about the dinner I had served, and felt that the Japanese would enjoy a cookbook that used Japanese ingredients in such an original way.

I was very flattered, but I told the publisher: "Although I love Japanese food, I cannot cook like the Japanese. Japanese cooking requires years of training and hours of preparation. I work in New York, and I

204

have no time to spend hours in the kitchen. What I like to do is to cook Japanese ingredients my way, but then serve them in the spirit of the Japanese cooking tradition. I would give them recipes that are different from what they are used to."

We discussed a book contract over the next two weeks. Finally it was decided that I was to come back to Japan at their expense and explore other Japanese cooking traditions. I thought, just for a minute, that my family and Jimmy would not be that pleased, but I said yes very quickly anyway.

I left Andre worried about his future. Later I was pleased to learn that Seibu had happily given him permission to use their gallery for the exhibition of French painters. The dinner had worked! However, a few months later he was recalled to Paris and resumed his career as a writer.

Back in New York I prepared myself for another trip to Japan, talking to Arakawa, Peter Grilli and other Japanese friends to plan my itinerary for the following June. I made a list of the cities that I wanted to visit.

The following June, 1989, I left once again for Tokyo. Upon my arrival I was visited by Hiroshi Tashigahara, the film maker I had met at the Arakawas'. I had loved his film, *Woman in the Dunes*. Hiroshi was also a master of flower arrangement and had a very successful school teaching young women this classical Japanese art. A few days after I arrived in Tokyo, Hiroshi asked me if I would do a friend of his a great favour. The friend had invested in several *crêperies*, but the business was failing and he wanted me to look at the restaurants to see why they were such a failure. For the next two days I visited the *crêperies* and realized immediately that the batter was wrong, and that the cooks had not learned how to make the perfect *crêpe*. I gathered all the cooks together in one of the restaurants, made a batter and taught them how to make a real French *crêpe*.

The next day the owner sent his manager to the hotel where I was staying. He handed me an envelope and said, bowing very low, "Please count the money. Mr O. is so pleased and thankful for your help." I refused the envelope, saying, "I did very little. Thank you, but there is no need." He insisted, and so I opened the envelope and nearly had a heart attack as I counted the money. There was the equivalent of thirty thousand dollars in my trembling hands. Bowing even lower, I thanked him and rushed to my room. I picked up the phone, called Jimmy, waking him up, and told him to take the first plane to Tokyo to join me, explaining briefly what had happened.

A few days later Jimmy arrived and together we travelled, eating our way through Tokyo, Kyoto and Osaka. Jimmy took pictures and I took notes on every dish we ate.

A year later, Jimmy told me that his firm was doing very well: "Thomas is graduating this spring. He'll be going to college in the autumn. We can manage without your teaching. Would you like to quit school and just write?"

This had been my dream for several years, and so the following June I resigned from my position at the school and said goodbye to all my teaching friends. I shed a tear or two, and with great trepidation and fear I looked forward to a year of not only writing, but also of travelling and writing about my travels too.

Chicken Liver Mousse

Clean 450g/1lb fresh chicken livers, removing fat and gristle. In a large skillet melt 2 tablespoons butter and sauté the livers for 3 minutes on each side. Sprinkle with salt and pepper and 1 tablespoon dry tarragon. Remove the livers and place in a food processor along with 2 eggs and 1 cup 220ml/8fl oz double cream. Process until all the ingredients are puréed. Strain the mixture through a fine sieve. Pour the strained and puréed livers into a 2 litre/4 pint soufflé dish. Place the soufflé dish in a baking tray and add 2 litres/4 pints of water to the pan to create a water bath. Bake in 180°C/350°F/gas mark 4 oven for 40 minutes. Remove from the oven and cool. Refrigerate until ready to serve. Serve with toasted baguette. Serves 8.

Sugar Snap Peas and Radish Salad

Snap the ends off 450g/1lb of sugar snap peas. Place the peas in a steamer and steam for 3 minutes. Refresh immediately under cold running water and drain. Cut the stems off 1 bunch of radishes and wash carefully. Pat dry and thinly slice. Place the sugar snap peas and the radishes in a salad bowl. In a small bowl mix together 3 tablespoons plain yogurt with 1 tablespoon lemon juice, salt and pepper and 2 tablespoons chopped fresh basil leaves. Mix well and pour over the salad. Toss and serve. Serves 4.

Dipping Sauce for Raw Vegetables

In a food processor place 225g/8oz spinach, stems removed, with 225g/8oz watercress, stems removed, 450g/1lb plain yogurt, the juice of half a lemon and 2 tablespoons olive oil. Process until all the ingredients are puréed. Remove to a bowl, add salt and pepper to taste and refrigerate until ready to serve.

Long Chinese String Beans

Cut the string beans into four. Place in a saucepan and cover with boiling water and 1 teaspoon salt. Bring to a boil, reduce the heat and cook for 8 minutes. Drain. In the same saucepan melt 2 tablespoons butter. Add 2 minced garlic cloves and 5 tablespoons chopped parsley, salt and pepper. Cook for 3 minutes stirring all the while then add the string beans, mix well and simmer for 4 minutes. Serve with roast chicken or steak.

Red Snapper with Cucumbers

Peel and slice very thinly 1 long oriental cucumber. Sprinkle with coarse salt and set aside on a plate for 20 minutes. Drain. Wash and pat dry about 900g/2lb of red snapper fillets. Line a bamboo steamer with lettuce leaves, place the fillets on top of the leaves and steam for 5 minutes. Remove the fillets to a platter and pour over the fish the juice of 2 limes. Set aside. In a bowl mix together 120g/4oz plain yogurt with 1 tablespoon strong Dijon mustard and 2 tablespoons chopped chives.

Pour the yogurt sauce over the fish, surround with the cucumbers and garnish with chopped parsley. Serves 4.

CHAPTER SEVEN

The Journalist

Every few years Jimmy gives me a wonderful present for my birthday: a bound book written and illustrated by him. Each of the books tells the story of what has happened to me in the last few years or decade, picking up where he left off the last time. Today, as I sat down to write, I picked up the 1979–89 book to look at his magnificent drawings. I flipped through the book and saw a drawing of me topless in an open bath house in Japan; a drawing of my daughter Marianne being married in our garden; a drawing of me writing in a tiny room, surrounded by hundreds of cookbooks.

By the autumn of 1988, I had stopped teaching at St Anne's in order to devote myself full time to writing. The first few weeks were difficult. I had to adjust to the fact that I did not have to get up at 6 a.m. in order to be at school at 8.30; that there were no children to take care of. Marianne was about to get married, and dreamed about becoming a teacher; Juliette was in Turkey teaching English to young Turkish girls, and Cecile was about to embark on an architectual career. As for Thomas, Jimmy and I had just driven him, our youngest child, to Dartmouth College. Now during the day the house was empty. I was free to do whatever I wanted. I did nothing for a few weeks; I roamed around the house aimlessly, thinking over and over, *What if I can't find anything to do? What if I have no ideas for stories? What if people forget me? What if the telephone never rings?* I was scared, lonely and missed the excitement of teaching and the conversation and laughter of my teacher friends. I missed the anticipation of creating new programmes. I missed running my department.

In order to prepare for my "new life" as a full-time writer, I began by organizing my space in the house. Until now, I'd had the smallest room in the house as my study. I decided to move my books and computer to one of the children's deserted bedrooms. The room was large and airy and I hated it. I missed the comfort of my compact office, and so I moved back. I tried to work but failed to write even a single line. I was experiencing not only the "empty nest" syndrome, but also a change in the way I looked at my work, and even at my life. For years I had taught because we needed the money. What I had really wanted to do was pushed aside simply out of necessity. But when the opportunity finally came my way I had to cope with too much change all at once. The same month I resigned from St Anne's, I had also lost my job at *New York Magazine*.

New York Magazine had been my lifeline to the food world. For years I had been writing short pieces for their Best Bets section. It had all started when I met Gael Green, the food editor of *New York Magazine* at a party in East Hampton. We had a lot in common, Gael and me. We both liked good food, we were both good cooks and, above all, we both liked to write about it.

One day I received a call from Gael. Would I be interested in becoming The "Underground Gourmet" restaurant reviewer for *New York Magazine?*

I had wanted to review restaurants for many years and this, I thought, would be the perfect job for me. Gael explained that the magazine was considering three other writers for this spot. The rules of the Underground Gourmet column were very strict. No main dish could cost more than $8.50, not an easy criterion to meet even in 1982. But I knew Chinatown and ethnic restaurants very well, so I was sure I could do the job. Gael suggested that I choose a restaurant and write a review.

I chose an Ethiopian restaurant on Thompson Street. I had two very close Ethiopian friends, and had eaten at their house several times. Also, I had been introduced to Ethiopian food on my visits to Africa and felt I knew it quite well. So I wrote my piece, got Jimmy to check it for English and grammar, and sent it in. A few weeks later, I was hired.

I worked as the Underground Gourmet reviewer for the next three years. I loved discovering small, new restaurants. I remember once walking down to visit the new South Street Seaport complex, which had just opened. I lost my way and ended up on a side street where I noticed a seafood restaurant advertising mussels, a whole bowl with Italian bread, for only $6. The restaurant was empty, the mussels were deliciously fresh, and when I spoke to the owner I was astonished to learn that he was a wholesale fishmonger at the Fulton Fish Market. He had always dreamed of opening a restaurant, and now he was trying to make a go of it but had not been entirely successful. I wrote the story and a few weeks later, passing by, I saw a line of customers waiting to be seated. Another discovery was a bistro called La Luncheonette on Essex Street, which was run by a Frenchman who was the cook, the waiter and the sommelier. A year after my story was published he moved his restaurant to Tenth Avenue, and was able to hire a waiter and a dishwasher. Success stories made me very proud.

Every year, apart from restaurant reviews, I worked on the "Round Up of New Restaurants" issue; stories on the best potato pancake in New York, the best barbecues, the best restaurants for takeaways, and many more. Writing these survey features was incredibly hard work. My writing was straightforward; very accurate and knowledgeable in describing the food or the decor, but I knew that it did not quite match the witty, trendy *New York Magazine* "new journalism" style. This would prove to be my downfall.

In 1988, Chinatown saw an explosion of new restaurants. Loaded with cash, Chinese were arriving in droves from Hong Kong. They were used to much better fare than the mushy meals served in New York's traditional Chinese restaurants which were geared to an imagined American taste. I suggested a piece on the best new restaurants in Chinatown. My piece would describe the many dishes new to New York. Everyone at the magazine agreed that this was a great idea, and I set out to select the top ten. I turned to my closest Chinese friend, Suzanne Chen, and Suzanne and I ate our way through Chinatown. I wrote my piece and presented my expense account. The editor-in-chief liked my story, but said that it lacked the New York Magazine voice. Furthermore, he added, he was astonished by my soaring expenses. "Look," he said, brandishing my expense account, "you say here that a bird's nest soup cost $30! That's outrageous!" He then pulled out of his desk drawer a soiled takeaway menu from the hole-in-the wall Chinese restaurant around the corner. "Look, a perfectly good bird's nest soup here is only five bucks. I'll pay you for the article but I won't reimburse your expense account. Take it or leave!"

I tried to explain that the bird's nest soup I had written about was the real thing. What he ate at his desk was just make-believe, a tasteless version. Refusing to back down, I walked out and thus lost the job I had loved more than any other.

So now I was a freelance journalist. I was not shy, but I found it very tough to knock on doors, and also at this point I had no idea of what I wanted to write. A chance encounter set me on the right track.

The food world was changing dramatically. The Greenmarket on Union Square, a farmers' market thought up by our friend Barry Benepe, was now offering chefs' ingredients previously available only in Europe or Asia, that local farmers were now growing on New York and New Jersey farms near the city. At the Greenmarket and in the new Korean produce stores,

214

herbs such as fresh pineapple mint, real French tarragon, purple basil or Greek oregano, and organic vegetables were becoming ordinary, daily fare. New Yorkers were now clamouring for better breads. Bakeries such as Our Daily Bread and the Sullivan Street Bakery were opening in many neighbourhoods in New York, offering French baguettes and croissants, and Italian *ciabatte* or *pugliese*. Dean & Deluca, Balducci's, Whole Foods and Gourmet Garage in the Village were a few of the pioneering stores where one shopped for unique ingredients from the world over.

SoHo had changed a great deal since we had bought our house in 1967. Up Sullivan Street from our house, Once Upon A Tart, the gourmet café run by Jerome, served small vegetarian *quiches*, scrumptious sandwiches and exotic salads along with excellent muffins, cheddar-dill scones (I was addicted to them), fruit tarts and rich, black French roast coffee. Around the corner on Prince Street, Luigi's was replaced by Raoul's, a hot French restaurant filled with beautiful people. It had just received a two-star rating from the *New York Times*. There were many new trendy boutiques such as Diesel Jeans, Hans Koch leather bags, a Tibetan silk and jewellery store and, most important, a 24-hour Korean greengrocers with a street-side flower shop at the corner of Thompson and Prince which changed the whole aspect of the street. But my favourite place was Dean & Deluca, a brilliant new grocery and produce store on Prince Street, just off West Broadway. The store was the brain-child of two men, Joel Dean who took care of the buying, and Jack Ceglic who designed the store. Added to this pair was a third man, an Italian, Georgio Deluca, whose main interest was cheeses from all over the world.

One day, walking down Prince Street, I stopped short in front of Dean & Deluca's window. I could not believe my eyes. It looked like a window from Fauchon's in Paris. Intrigued, I entered the store to talk to Joel Dean who had designed the window, and he introduced me to Lee Grimsbo. Lee was a tall, young, laconic man with a shy smile. He came from the Midwest, and was the son of a biologist who had interested him in the cultivation of organic fruit and vegetables. What Lee wanted most in life, he told me, was to share his knowledge with the public and at the same time help his friends. I liked Lee; we had the same goals. Every day I would stop by the store and talk to him, asking what new vegetable or fruit he had. He brought in cardoons that the Italians had eaten for centuries; he showed me a Romanesco cauliflower from Holland, a cross between cauliflower and broccoli. I would go to my kitchen, try his vegetables, and come back to him with recipes I thought he could share with his customers.

One day Lee asked me why I hadn't written a story about the revolution in the agricultural world in the United States. He suggested a trip around the country where he would introduce me to all his friends. I asked an old friend, Philip Herrera, then managing editor of *Connoisseur Magazine*, if he would be interested in such a piece. Philip talked to Tom Hoving, the

216

editor-in-chief, and my story got the go-ahead: they were willing to pay for the trip.

In early June, Lee and I flew to San Francisco where we visited several of Lee's farmer friends. Most of them were in their twenties, did not come from farming families, and had degrees in subjects such as English Literature, Chemistry and Engineering. Bored with the prospect of futures as engineers and scientists, they had decided to buy a few acres and start farming. A few told me that Alice Waters of Chez Panisse restaurant had inspired them to grow vegetables such as ramps, the wild onion, or fiddleheads ferns from the banks of brooks. Some had begun to grow delicate miniature vegetables. Others visited Europe and came back with seeds for patty pan squash, miniature zucchini, and five different kinds of potato; one or two brought back purple potatoes from Peru.

We then drove through California — the Napa Valley and Sonoma Valley — meeting with young hippies who cultivated very large gardens.

A month later we flew to Florida, which had also become an innovative agricultural centre. There we met more young farmers trying new varieties of fruit and vegetables.

My piece became a cover story for *Connoisseur*, and I was delighted by the accompanying photographs which made the vegetables look like precious jewels. The success of the story led to other plum assignments. I wrote about the new farmers' markets which had sprung up all over the country, and I did another story for *Connoisseur* on the century-old Lexington Market in Baltimore. For *Metropolitan Home* I wrote on San Michele de Allende in Mexico, and about Chinatown's nouvelle cuisine for *Elle Magazine*.

I also worked for two years for *McCall's Magazine* as their food and design editor. Working for a magazine as an editor was a new experience and very exciting, and it led to being asked to create a new magazine for the Midwest. Like most new ventures in the publishing world this was short-lived. Once again I turned to freelance work, never really finding a niche that made me happy.

Later, when my eldest daughter Marianne was expecting her first child, she was searching for something to do. She suggested a collaboration; together we would write a vegetable cookbook which would be a dialogue between mother and daughter. We travelled to farmers' markets, invented recipes, hired the photographer Greg Sclight, and did the food styling ourselves. The book, *Vegetables*, was published in 1991. It was wild and fun, Craig Claiborne loved it, and so did the rest of the food press. As a mother and daughter team we appeared on TV and radio. But then Marianne wanted to go back to college and our collaboration ended.

I felt restless, nervous, and even bored. *What was happening to me?* I was always on the go, and most of the time, I wanted to be out of the house. In reality I wanted to leave Jimmy for a little while. I needed to get away. I loved him but I couldn't stand hearing about his office problems and his money worries every night. I was changing. I wanted something different, but what?

I tried to explain it to Jimmy but found it difficult. I thought we both had to think about the future. Jimmy needed to think about his own future. Architecture, planning cities, or painting? Which one to choose? I thought that, if I went away, he could manage better and see his future more clearly. And maybe I would to.

One day I read a short article in one of the French magazines I subscribed to. The story was about an Australian who had saved a group of camels who were roaming the desert of Australia. Apparently, in the 1990s, the Australian government had the camels brought in from Afghanistan, so that a surveying party could be sent out to map the vast desert. Once the mapping was done the camels were abandoned. They multiplied and multiplied. The government was about to exterminate them as a nuisance when a young man named Peter S. decided to step in. He went to Afghanistan to learn all about camels. Now it seemed he was trying to start camel-trekking expeditions through the desert for tourists. His idea was that trekkers would ride across the desert on camels, visiting watering holes and Aborigine villages. This sounded very exciting and an answer to my problems. I thought I should pursue the story.

I called the travel editor of the *New York Times* and suggested a story idea: a middle-aged woman on a camel trek across the desert of Australia. She accepted it, and for the next three weeks I planned the trip.

I visited the Australian Tourist Bureau, talked with their representative and made an itinerary that would take me from Cairns in the north to Alice Springs, where I would meet Peter S. for the camel trek, and then go on to Sidney and Melbourne.

Alice Springs is located in the heart of the Australian desert and is the home of the famous Ayers Rock, or *Uluru* in Aborigine. This enormous pinkish-grey monolith dominates thirty-six other domed rocks, and together they are a very important part of Aboriginal religious belief. I wanted to visit Ayers Rock, but after a quick look had to leave for the camel ranch.

Peter S., the camel trainer, had built a very primitive ranch in the desert. There were a few bedrooms with crude showers, a bar, and a simple restaurant for the locals. I looked for Peter in the bar which was filled with men in blue jeans and boots drinking beer. A man of about thirty-five, tall, blond and wearing heavy boots, approached me and asked what I wanted.

"I'm here to meet someone called Peter S."

"I'm Peter."

Staring at me, a short, middle-aged lady, he suddenly blurted out:

"I was really expecting a young woman."

I didn't know how to answer, but said:

"Don't worry, I grew up in Egypt; I know all about camels."

Relieved, Peter explained that everything was ready and that we could leave at dawn the next morning. We were going to travel on camels for five days, ending up in an Aborigine village where the head of the council had agreed to house me for a night. During the camel trek, we would sleep in the open air and wash and swim in waterholes. Peter would do the cooking.

That morning I followed Peter to the Camel Corral. Peter brought out five camels: one for me, one for him, one for a helper who he introduced as John, no last name. John was a scrawny fellow with long, dirty-blond sideburns. The two other camels were going to be laden with sleeping bags, cooking utensils, and food and water for the next four days. Once on the camel's back, I realized that in Egypt I had really never travelled very far. Faced with five uncomfortable hours, I regretted my boast. The camels followed one another in a single file; there was really no good way to talk. This would be a silent trip. I looked around me. The sand was the colour of ochre. From time to time I saw a colourful bird flying away as we approached. The flora and the fauna were very different from that in France or the US or East Africa. There were some acacia trees, smaller than the ones I knew at home; there were also eucalyptus trees, whose smell reminded me of our Cairo garden.

At noon, Peter halted the camels and announced that it was time for lunch. Lunch was ham sandwiches downed with the local beer. Slightly tipsy, I went back on my camel for another five-hour ride. The sun had come out; the colour of the sand was changing. I saw wild flowers that I hadn't noticed before, red flowers with dark black centres, pink ones with white edges, and a strange, spiky plant that Peter told me later would bloom after the first rain.

During those five hours, I daydreamed. I thought of work, home, my children, Jimmy. I felt totally at peace with myself, and very content.

When we finally stopped riding, Peter and John made a fire and cooked. They broiled some steaks, made bread and served some salad. For dessert we had fruit and cookies. We drank lots of beer, sang songs and told stories. They asked about New York, my family, and women. Around nine Peter announced that we had to sleep as the following day we would ride to the first waterhole.

The next day we arrived at an enormous hole in the middle of the desert filled with clear blue water. Peter told me to undress and swim, it would refresh me. He added that for the next hour he and John would go for a walk. And so I bathed in the coolest and most refreshing water I had ever experienced.

Then it was my turn to go for a walk while they bathed. I walked towards a baobab tree. I hadn't seen one since Tanzania. The hole of its trunk was full of water, and there were multi-coloured birds drinking from it. I saw lizards at least twenty inches long, gliding on the sand, and small rodents running around. The colour of the sand was continually changing from a light pink to dark ochre. The desert was varied and incredibly beautiful, nothing like the one I knew outside Cairo, where for miles you saw nothing but yellow sand.

For the next two days we went from waterhole to waterhole, finally reaching our goal, the Aborigine village.

The head or chief of the village was a woman, a tall giant of a woman with black hair and large black eyes. She wore a skirt and a wool sweater torn at the elbows.

The village was formed of austere square concrete houses with a central communal building and a school near the edge of the settlement. The village looked very poor, and it was.

That night, dinner was served under a baobab tree. The women and children sat in a circle around a fire that an elder had built. A woman was roasting what looked liked very large corn kernels.

"Peter, what are these?"

"These are grubs, large silk worms that grow in the roots of the trees around here. They're really delicious. Babies and young children are fed raw ones and the adults eat them cooked over charcoal."

And picking one up with a metal fork he handed it over to me. It did taste like roasted corn and was very good. I asked for more, the women laughed and seemed pleased that I liked their food. We ate Peter's bread with dark, red berries, drank beer and listened to an Aborigine man blowing on a long, wooden flute. "It's a didgeridoo," explained Peter, "the oldest instrument on earth." The sound was in a low pitch, something like the soft moan of a bird. While he played the women and children sang. Their song told the story of the desert, of hunting and of animals. It was just beautiful and very sad.

We left the next morning. This time we took a short cut and reached the camel ranch in only a day and a half. Exhausted but pleased that I had survived, I flew to Sydney. The next two weeks went like a dream. I felt energized by my trekking trip. I had thought a lot about what I wanted to do: I was going to write about my trip

and then write about the Aborigine village and the courageous woman who ran it.

During the trek I had often thought of Jimmy. I realized how much I loved him and how lonely I was without him. He was not only my husband and lover, but he was also my best friend. I longed to see him. I felt that from now on we should share every thing, work and play.

Back in New York Jimmy picked me up from the airport and we drove home.

"I missed you. How was your trip? You look great."

"I missed you too and I love you, but I'm tired. Give me a day and I'll tell you all about it. Such an exciting country!"

I wrote the trekking story, and I kept in touch with the Aborigine village and Peter. His trekking venture was slowly picking up, and he hoped that soon he could hire more help.

Six months later I was asked to write a story on Corsica for *European Travel* magazine. This time I insisted that Jimmy come with me: "You have a better eye. You see things I don't. We will be together." When he agreed I felt good and full of energy.

Upon my return I started a column, "Ask Colette", for the *Daily News*. I loved writing this column, and I would receive about twenty letters a week. Some were from older women who would ask me about recipes that they used to cook but now, older and alone, had forgotten how to prepare them. Others were from younger women who wanted to reproduce for their own children dishes that their mothers or grandmothers had

made for them. There were letters from men who just felt lonely and wanted to correspond with someone. They wrote that my replies were like me chatting with them in the kitchen. Once I even got a letter from a prisoner who read my column and wanted a recipe for clam bake. He wrote that as soon as he was out he would prepare one and invite me to share it with him. After publishing the recipe I never got my invitation or heard from him again. I wrote this column for ten years, until the spring of 2004.

Mizuma Tea Sandwiches

Trim the crust of 1 white loaf of bread, thinly sliced. Wash half a *mizuma* (Japanese salad grown in California) and pat dry with paper towel. Coarsely chop 120g/4oz of smoked salmon. Add the salmon to 225g/8oz of cream cheese and mix well with a fork. Spread the cream cheese mixture on half the bread slices. Top with the *mizuma* leaves and cover with a slice of bread. Cut each sandwich diagonally and stack, pyramid fashion on a serving platter. Cover the sandwiches with a damp kitchen towel or seal with cling film until ready to serve. The *mizuma* can be substituted by chopped watercress.

Steamed Flowering Kale with Veal

Cut 450g/1lb of thinly sliced veal into thin strips. Twist each strip and bring the ends together to form a circle. Attach with a toothpick. Dust the circles lightly with

225

flour. In a skillet heat 4 tablespoons of oil. When the oil is hot add 3 chopped garlic cloves, sauté until golden, then add the veal circles and sauté quickly, turning just once until golden brown. Sprinkle with salt and pepper. Transfer the veal to a hot platter. Remove the outer leaves of a large flowering kale. Steam the kale for 10 minutes or until tender. Place the kale on a large platter and sprinkle with salt. With kitchen shears cut several leaves and arrange on individual plates like the petals of a flower. Remove the toothpicks from the veal circles. Place in the centre several veal circles. Sprinkle the dish with pink peppercorns and chopped coriander. Drizzle with olive oil and serve. Serves 4.

Braised Cardoons with Clementines

Cardoons are an edible thistle that look like overgrown celery and taste more like an artichoke. Remove the first layer of stalks from one medium bunch of cardoons. Cut each stalk into 1-inch pieces. In a large saucepan bring 2 litres/4 pints chicken stock to a boil with 1 tablespoon lemon juice. Add the cardoon pieces and lower the heat to medium. Cook the cardoons for 15 minutes. Drain and refresh under cold running water. Drain again. Remove any visible strings from the cardoons and peel. In a saucepan melt 4 tablespoons butter. When the butter is foamy add the cardoons, 1 tablespoon lemon juice, salt and pepper and 1 teaspoon dried sage. Lower the heat and cook for 30 minutes or until tender.

Meanwhile cut 4 clementines in half across the middle and remove any pips. In a large skillet melt 120g/4oz sugar with 60ml/2fl oz of water. Just before the sugar begins to colour add the clementines, 4 halves at a time and cook for 5 minutes, turning them once so that they are glazed all over. Transfer the clementines with a slotted spoon onto a sheet of aluminum foil. Place the cardoons on a serving platter. Sprinkle with 1 tablespoon chopped parsley and surround with the glazed clementines. Serves 4.

Sautéd Fiddlehead Ferns with Pomegranate

Place 450g/1lb fiddleheads in a large bowl of cold water and lightly rub them with your hands to remove any brown layer. Drain and pat dry. Cut one ripe pomegranate in two over a bowl to catch the juice and remove the ruby red seeds. In a large skillet melt 2 tablespoons butter. Add the fiddleheads and cook over a medium heat for about 4 to 6 minutes. Sprinkle with salt and pepper and add 1–2 tablespoons chopped fresh tarragon. Mix well and place the fiddleheads in a bowl. Add 4 tablespoons of pomegranate seeds and mix well. Serve with roast pork or chicken. Serves 4.

Sprinkle the remaining pomegranate seeds with 3 tablespoons granulated sugar and refrigerate. Serve the next day with crème fraîche.

Spaghetti Squash with Cranberries

Cut 1 medium-sized spaghetti squash in two lengthways. Scoop out and discard the seeds. Place the squash in a large saucepan, add water to cover, cover the saucepan and bring to a boil. Then lower the heat to medium. Cook until tender, about 20 minutes. Melt 2 tablespoons butter in a saucepan. Add 1 heaped tablespoon of finely chopped fresh ginger and 1 heaped tablespoon of finely chopped shallots. Sauté until the shallots are soft, and then add 350g/12oz of fresh cranberries, 450ml/4fl oz of water and 3 tablespoons sugar. Bring the mixture to a boil, season with salt and pepper and cook, stirring occasionally until the sauce is thick. Drain the spaghetti squash and remove the flesh with a fork. Place the spaghetti squash in a large serving bowl and top with the cranberry sauce. Serve with roast chicken. Serves 4.

Green Grape Tart

Make some shortcrust pastry dough. Butter a 9-inch flan dish and dust with flour. Line the dish with the dough and crimp the edges. Prick the dough with a fork, line with greaseproof paper and fill with raw rice to prevent the dough from rising. Bake in 190°C/375°F/gas mark 5 oven for 30 minutes. Remove from the oven and cool. Discard the rice and the paper.

In a food processor place 4 egg yolks and 2 egg whites, 4 tablespoons flour, 75g/2½ oz of sugar, 450ml/4fl oz milk, 60ml/2fl oz double cream, 1 tablespoon brandy and 75g/2½ oz chopped almonds. Process for 30 seconds.

Pour the mixture into a saucepan and cook over a medium heat stirring all the while until the sauce thickens and coats a wooden spoon. Remove from the heat and cool.

Place 280g/10oz sugar in a saucepan with 180ml/6fl oz of water and cook over a medium heat, stirring constantly until the sugar has completely dissolved and turns a golden colour. Remove from the heat.

Remove 750g/1¾lb seedless grapes from their stems and wash. Drain and pat dry. Pour the cream mixture over the the pastry. Place the grapes in concentric circles on top and brush with the melted sugar. Refrigerate until ready to serve. Serves 6.

CHAPTER
EIGHT

My Family

I returned from my travels to take stock of my family. All of our children were at turning points in their lives.

Thomas had graduated from Dartmouth and went on to Harvard to study Architecture. There he fell in love with a fellow student who was studying law. Thomas and Rebecca waited until they both settled in New York before announcing that they were getting married.

After graduating from New York University, Marianne had decided to make a film which illustrated a poem by Edgar Allan Poe. The film was awarded a first prize for young directors in Paris and she elected to stay there and make another film. Soon she announced that she was in love with a Frenchman. They got married in New York and settled here, and it wasn't very long before she announced to our delight that she was expecting our first grandchild. We were blissfully happy.

Jimmy became more and more unhappy with his firm and his partnership. Bill Conklin, his partner, had become more interested in Peruvian textiles and was thinking of moving to Washington DC where he could work closely with the Textile Museum, and he and

Jimmy had drifted apart. Jimmy wanted a smaller firm with fewer financial problems, so they both decided to dissolve the partnership.

Jimmy moved his office to the two top floors of our house. Now with Thomas and Cecile, we had three architects in the family. Jimmy decided his new firm would be called 3R Architects, just in case any of them cared to join him and work with him. After finishing his studies, my nephew John had gone to work for *Business Week* and was now living in Rome, where he was *Business Week* bureau chief. He had met a beautiful Calabrese woman who was working for the Italian Ministry of Foreign Affairs. Antonella and John were married by the Mayor of Rome in a castle they had rented. Their wedding, which I catered, was the talk of the town.

And me? I was once again looking for a steady job. One day I saw an ad in the *New York Times*: A large French bank was looking for someone to teach their American vice-presidents French. I was interviewed and landed the job. My work was child's play after all my years of teaching. I taught executives who needed to learn enough French to be able to understand their French counterparts and read memos that came from Paris. The salary was high, and I had ample time left to write articles.

One night I was invited to dinner by Karin Bakoum, an old friend, half-Egyptian like me. We always joked that we were the only two Egyptian witches in New York as we claimed that we could read people's futures. At the table sat the editor of *Saveur* magazine. Karin was telling stories about me, how I was a witch too, at least that's what I went around telling everybody. Laughing, I told stories about growing up in Egypt, about fortune tellers and my Egyptian grandmother's great food.

A few days later I received a telephone call from *Saveur* magazine. Would I be interested in writing a story about growing up in Egypt, what my life was like and especially what the food was like? I eagerly accepted and went to work. I taught in the morning at the bank and in the evening wrote my story and tested the food. Six months after it was published I was nominated for the James Beard Award. I didn't win but the story, once expanded, became my first book of memoirs *Apricots on the Nile*.

My mother was now seventy-five, still looking as beautiful and as elegant as ever. When she had moved to New York after my stepfather's death, she quickly got bored. My children were in school all day long and we didn't need her as a babysitter very often. One day she announced that she had taken a job as a sales person at Lord & Taylor department store. She was working in the bridal department and all the future brides adored her. She loved her job and had made many friends.

At seventy she stopped working at Lord & Taylor and registered for courses at the Art Studio school. She wanted to paint. She had painted when she was young, before she was married. All the students, young and old, loved her. If the weather was bad and she could not make her classes, they would call to see how she was or take her out for coffee or lunch. She was also making friends with the older women in a St Anthony's parish whom she met at bingo games on Thursday nights and after mass on Sundays. They loved her, and they talked to me about the way she dressed, her hats and her lovely accent. They thought she was a great lady.

"You're so lucky to have her," they would say to me when I met them in the street. "Such a lovely lady." I couldn't understand them. Who was this woman they liked so much? This woman who, when I was child, had abandoned me for five years; who never had seemed to care about me.

My children loved her. The girls loved to hear her talk about the past when she was a rich young woman. She would show them photographs of her in a silk dress with pearls and a small dog on her lap. She would talk about her wedding:

"It was the wedding of the year," she would tell them proudly. "The house was full of flowers, we had four hundred guests. Your grandfather gave me a diamond brooch on our wedding day . . . We had our honeymoon in Venice."

"Grandmaman, tell us how you met him."

"Well, my best friend at the *lycée* was an Egyptian girl. She was engaged to Mendes France. You know, he became Prime Minister of France. I was invited to the wedding and your grandfather was there. He was asked to choose which of these young bridesmaids he would like to walk down the aisle. Guess who he picked? Me! We were married six months later."

My daughters enjoyed her stories and spent hours looking at her wedding pictures! And I would be ignored!

Then I started to notice that my mother was losing weight. She had been on diets most of her adult life, but now she suddenly looked too thin. She tired more easily, and often when I came to visit she would be either asleep in her chair near the window or sleeping in bed. It wasn't like her. I was still often angry with my mother because she refused to talk about the past, but I wanted her around me despite everything. I insisted that she see a doctor.

After a series of tests the news came in: she had advanced ovarian cancer and was dying. I wanted her to live. She was my last tie to my past. She had the memories, I didn't. She was going to die and I still did not know why she had deserted me years earlier. I wanted to know what her life had been like those years when she had left me? What had made her change? I tried to talk to her, but to her last breath she refused. She had built a past that existed only in her mind. She kept on talking about my children, not me. The only personal thing she confided in me was what should happen when she died. She told me that she wanted her ashes to be thrown into the ocean so that they would float back to France. She died one night alone in the hospital. Strangely, I felt relieved. There were no more questions to ask.

For weeks I put off fulfilling her last wishes. Then one day, alone, I took her ashes and boarded the ferry to Staten Island. In the middle of the trip I went on deck, looked around, and threw the box into the water, hoping it would float towards France.

That night Alan Buchsbaum came to visit. Alan was my best friend, always there when I needed to talk about my problems. We talked about my mother. Like everyone else, Alan liked my mother, and that night he made me laugh recalling how the two of them would share recipes or talk about opera.

"Let's have dinner," Alan suggested cheerfully. "When I'm sad it's food I need, comfort food."

We all ended up in the kitchen to cook dinner. Alan prepared his favourite dish, baked grits with cheese, and I sautéd chicken breast with lots of garlic and parsley. As the cooking aroma wafted through the kitchen, I began to feel better. As when I was a little girl, food, once again, was helping me cope with my pain.

But an unexpected loss would shatter our lives.

One night Alan, who had recently returned from a trip to Senegal with a friend, came for dinner and brought me a lovely present, a set of ivory bracelets. He looked tired, but then I assumed it was just jet lag. We chatted about his trip, my work and the cooking school he had helped create. He talked about Senegalese food, soups and stews he had loved and would cook for me in the following weeks. I didn't see Alan for a few months. I kept on calling him, inviting him over, but he kept on getting the flu, or at least this is what he said he had. I asked him to come and live with us for a while so that I could take care of him. He refused: "I'll be fine. I have friends who help me and I have to work. Let's have dinner together here as soon as my cold is over."

A few weeks later, when I called his office to invite him once again for dinner, I was told that he had pneumonia and was in hospital. I went to see him, but when I got there I was led to a special hospice-like part of the hospital. Alan was segregated with other patients who, like him, had pneumonia. He lay in his bed, pale, his eyes closed, looking so sick. I wanted to cry.

Then I heard him say in a very low voice, "Water, I'm thirsty." I saw no glass, only long, very large Q-tips. I went out and asked the nurse what to do.

"With Aids patients, you take the Q-tips, soak them in water and wet their lips. Don't touch anything, don't touch him and wash your hands."

This is how I learned that Alan had Aids. It explained his flu symptoms and his tiredness. I was horrified and sad. I was aware of the disease which had been spreading, but Aids hadn't been made real for me until that day. I tiptoed back to his room, did as the nurse had told me, and as I was wetting his lips he opened his eyes, looked at me and murmured, "Go, go, leave me." After a few minutes I left.

I realized, thinking back, that Alan had never wanted me to know he was gay. Despite our lasting friendship he didn't think I would approve. He was so wrong. I had known for years and was completely comfortable with him. We flirted but I knew it was all a game. I trusted him — he was my best friend. I felt sad, and also betrayed as he had not trusted me.

I called the hospital every day to see how he was but he never wanted to speak to me. Once he was back home and feeling better, he came by to see me. Once again we cooked together, talked together, but he never mentioned my visit to the hospital and I didn't know what I was supposed to say or do.

A few months later, Alan was back at the hospice. This time both Jimmy and I came right away. When Jimmy left the room, I sat down near him and told him I knew he was gay, that it made no difference to me, that I was his friend, that he had to trust me.

"I am sorry Colette, you must forgive me. This is very hard. I hate what this disease is doing to me. I don't want to die . . ."

I was brokenhearted to see him like this. We had been so close to him, and we knew his mother and sister. Years ago, when I wanted to write about Savannah, he had helped me. We stayed with his family. I felt he was like my brother. I was losing my best friend to this horrible disease that would take so many lives in the years that followed.

A few days later Alan died. There was a memorial service for him and half of SoHo came, including celebrities for whom he had designed apartments or lofts. Both Marianne and Juliette wrote and read poems. Of all our children, Marianne was the most affected. They had been close and when she had a problem with a relationship, instead of talking with us, she went to him for advice. He would then help me to understand what was happening to Marianne. Alan's death was a great loss for the whole family, and Jimmy and I became more involved in our children's lives. We wanted to protect them from the outside world. We tried to stop them getting too hurt as they joined the adult world. Looking back, I realize that I was too involved in their lives then and often interfered, trying to solve their problems when I should have been letting go of my children. Despite that, like many other couples in these troubled times, we sometimes failed, but we still managed to remain a close-knit family.

Juliette, always the most adventurous, had gone to Turkey to teach. While in Istanbul, Juliette had managed to get Jimmy an exciting new architectural job, the design of a new gymnasium for her school. While the gymnasium was being built we went several times to Turkey to visit.

On her days off, Juliette and I explored the bazaar, ate in small restaurants and visited markets. My Egyptian grandmother was born in Istanbul and I felt very at home there.

But Juliette soon grew bored with teaching English to wealthy Turkish girls, and later college students, and decided to become a journalist. It was during the time of the first Gulf War, and because she was fluent in Turkish, she was hired by *Business Week*. Her first big break came when she covered the war on the Turkish-Iraqi border. She wrote from Cizre about the plight of the Kurds who were crossing the border from Iraq into Turkey. When the war was over, she reported on the Kurdish refugee camps where hundreds were dying. She also had a by-line for the *New York Post*. I would learn about her exploits by reading the paper.

When the war was over, Juliette continued to write for *Business Week*. She covered the war in Azerbaijan, the former Soviet republic in the Caucasus. She sent dispatches about a fierce battle between Armenians and Azerbaijanis as witnessed from a helicopter under fire. We learned all of this through her articles, living in fear that something terrible might happen to her.

At the same time she was falling in and out of love. First she fell deeply in love with a Turkish teacher, but this didn't work out. Later she fell in love with a French journalist who whisked her away to Moscow. This didn't work out either but Juliette, still the great adventurer, learned Russian and witnessed the Russian uprising in Moscow and the burning of the Russian "White House". From Russia she took many trips to Central Asia, to Turkmenistan, Kazakhstan and Uzbekistan. To our great relief she came back to New York in one piece and started to work for *Forbes Magazine*. She had fallen in love with a bright American who was working in Saudi Arabia. David spoke Arabic and loved the Middle East. Marriage was in the air and we felt very happy for her.

But it was Cecile who we were most worried about. She had taken years to decide what she wanted to do and finally followed Jimmy's footsteps and studied architecture. After graduating as an architect from Princeton, Cecile had a problem finding work; New York was in a recession and work for young architects was sparse. She worked for Jimmy's office for a few months, then for Arakawa, our artist friend. When Arata Isozaki, a Japanese architect and our friend, came to

New York, he told Arakawa he needed young architects for his office in Tokyo. Arakawa suggested he hire Cecile, and so for a while Cecile worked at Arata's New York office and then left for Tokyo to join the main office.

Much later, Jimmy was offered a spring show of his drawings at a prestigious gallery in Tokyo. We flew to Tokyo for the opening and spent time with Cecile. After a week I was sad to leave Cecile alone again in Japan, but very soon letters and e-mails arrived full of good news. Cecile loved Japan, was learning the language very fast and was having a very creative time. By the autumn, she had met a young Japanese architect and was deeply in love. The following Christmas they both arrived in New York. Ghen was a handsome and gracious man who loved music and art. He seemed to be a very talented architect, and most of all he loved Cecile. We were delighted to have them with us. When they were about to leave, being an interfering mother, I asked Ghen if was going to marry Cecile. His answer was, "I ask her every day, but she says she is happy as we are."

A month later Cecile called. "We're getting married. But the wedding has to be in Japan because Ghen's grandfather is too old to come to New York and Ghen wants him to be present. You don't have to do anything. We're designing the wedding."

Cecile had been our most restless child and we were ecstatic that she had finally found someone who shared her ideas about life. Although disappointed that the wedding would not take place in New York, and that once married they would continue to live in Japan, in my mind I was planning future trips back and forth.

A few weeks before the wedding we were woken at two in the morning by a telephone call from Cecile. Ghen had died suddenly in her arms. The cause was a brain aneurysm. We learned to our horror that she had tried to get help from neighbours but doors were slammed in her face, and when the ambulance had finally arrived it was too late.

The next morning I flew to Japan to be with her. What do you say to your child when her world collapses? When you look at her and see how deep the hurt is? You say nothing, you are simply there. You hold her hands, you let her cry and stay by her side. The funeral was long and arduous. I stayed a week longer than I'd intended. I hated leaving her alone in the tiny apartment she had shared with Ghen. I wanted her back with us but she adamantly refused. She was staying in Japan.

Months went by. Every time I called I could hear the tears in her voice. I had to help her get out of Japan. Jimmy and I decided that we would talk to Arata Isozaki. I knew in my heart that I should not interfere, but I could not stand her pain and thought, right or wrong, that once out of Japan where everything reminded her of Ghen, she might feel better. Arata was an internationally renowned architect who had projects around the world. We begged him to send Cecile somewhere, anywhere, but away from Japan. A few months later Cecile announced that Arata Isozaki was sending her to Berlin to help with the building of a large project. Cecile had been in Berlin for two years when she told us before Christmas that she was visiting us with a new wonderful friend. Christian, her future husband, came into our lives and we hoped that Cecile had recovered from Ghen's death and would be able to rebuild her life.

Meanwhile Matthew, our first grandchild, was born. Two years later, Marianne announced she was pregnant again, and Thomas and Rebecca were married. Juliette was seriously in love with David. They got married in Jordan, but they were moving back to New York. A few months later Julien, Marianne's second little boy, was born. The family was growing.

Two years after Julien was born, Marianne divorced and was living in Brooklyn with her two little boys. She had become very involved in education, and was now taking a degree in the subject at the New School University. She had decided on a teaching career and wanted to help create the new, radical, smaller schools that were her dream. She had met a young man, Edi, who shared her dreams. Together, once she'd graduated, they would move to Santa Barbara, California.

Thomas was designing very exciting projects at a leading New York firm, while being totally absorbed by his lovely baby son Luca.

Cecile married Christian and stayed in Berlin. She was still working as an architect but had also begun to write a book of short stories. Her daughter Celine was saying her first words of English, and soon Cecile was also expecting her second child.

242

Meanwhile our house on Sullivan Street was changing. Our children had flown the coop and the house seemed deserted, too vast for both of us. Jimmy decided to remodel it.

"Let's build an apartment downstairs. It will bring us much-needed income." I protested. I loved my house, my garden. I would lose my kitchen and dining room. But Jimmy promised to build me a new kitchen, better than the one I had downstairs, and a dining room with a copper dome. "A *tempieto*," he called it, "a small temple of food, just for you."

So for a month we camped in a house under construction, going back to our beginnings, often cooking in the fireplace while the new kitchen was being built. Jimmy was very excited about this project; it was the first time he was designing and building something new for us. He spent hours with the contractors, often changing the design. I would get upset as my lovely garden was trampled by the construction workers. Also I got very impatient, asking every day when the work would be finished.

Then one day the project *was* finished and the downstairs apartment was ready to be rented. The *tempieto* was lovely, full of light, with a great view of the garden. The kitchen was ready and, once again, I started to cook inspired by my *tempieto* filled with light. We threw an enormous housewarming party and all of New York seemed to be there. Friends, children, and grandchildren's laughter filled the house, a flowering hibiscus grew on the kitchen balcony and my roses bloomed once again.

It is Christmas Eve and all our children are gathered in our SoHo town house. Two days ago Thomas and I went to buy a Christmas tree. Tonight we will decorate it with Christmas ornaments that we have accumulated over the years. My favourites are the ones we bought when our children were very young on our trip to Guatemala. They are made of straw, but look like gold in the glow of the tiny Christmas lights. There are other charming ornaments that our friends have brought us. For the past twenty years we have given a party, inviting our friends to be with our children and grandchildren. Every guest has had to bring something for the tree. I usually ask that they make it, but they seldom do. Around midnight we serve dinner; I call it a *reveillon*, like the French. I serve a four-meat *pâté, boudin blanc* (a veal sausage served with good mustard), lentils with lots of garlic, salad, cheese, tangerines and a *bûche de Noël* (yule-log) that Jerome, the *patissier* from Once Upon a Tart down the street makes every year. After midnight, when all the guests have left, we bring the presents down from hiding places upstairs. Jimmy and Marianne have usually made the best packages. One year, the year the astronauts went to the moon, Jimmy transformed all the gifts into an enormous space ship. Another year he and Thomas built the city of Bethlehem, with palm trees decorated with little lights behind the village.

I am always in charge of the stockings. This is what I like best. I roam the city choosing small, amusing, unusual and often useless presents to fill them with. I hang them, one for each of the seventeen members of the family, on our mantelpiece. They are the first things we open in the morning before we have breakfast. The screams of delight of my grandchildren still resonate in my mind. Jimmy prepares breakfast. He is famous for his waffles. Since we've been married, now fifty years, Jimmy has always cooked breakfast on Christmas morning.

Christmas dinner is late at night. We all cook together. Marianne usually makes a soup. She makes a wonderful, pungent carrot and ginger soup. Thomas and I roast a goose and I stuff the neck following my French grandmother's very old recipe. Juliette takes care of dessert and Cecile, who is vegetarian half the time, cooks the vegetables. On this day, it is the only time when no one argues. Food in our family still seems to be the catalyst for bringing us together. We all sit, seventeen of us around a long table in the living room. It is the only time we eat there. As I look around the table I remember that as a child I never experienced this pleasure. Perhaps I have succeeded in my quest to create a real family, something I never had.

Carrot Soup

Peel, scrape and cut into 1-inch pieces 6 carrots. Place the carrots in a saucepan and cover with water and ½ teaspoon salt. Bring to a boil, lower the heat and cook for 15 minutes or until the carrots are done. Drain the carrots, reserving the liquid. Place the carrots in a food processor with 1 medium onion, a 2-inch piece of ginger, peeled and cut, 1 tablespoon dried thyme and 2 garlic cloves. Add 225ml/8fl oz of the carrot water and purée. In a saucepan bring to a boil 1.3 litres/2½ pints of chicken stock. Add the carrot purée and mix well. Correct the seasoning with salt and freshly ground pepper. Heat the soup then pour it in 6 individual bowls. Top with 1 tablespoon crèmé fraîche and garnish with 1 mint leaf. Serves 6.

Anne's Brisket of Beef

Ask your butcher to trim most of the fat of a 2.25kg/5lb beef brisket. Peel 6 garlic cloves and insert into the meat slivers of garlic. Place the meat in a large baking pan. Sprinkle with coarse salt and freshly ground pepper and 2 tablespoons of dried marjoram and thyme. Pour 2 tablespoons dark soy mixed with 2 tablespoons of olive oil on the meat. Peel and thinly slice 2 medium onions. Spread the slices on top of the meat. Then add 800ml/1½ pints of beef consommé to the pan. Cover the roasting pan with foil and bake at 180°C/350°F/gas mark 4 for 3 hours, adding more consommé if necessary. Remove the meat from the pan and thinly slice. Serve with the pan juices.

Kreplach

These kreplach are made with leftover brisket. In a bowl mix together 280g/10oz of flour with ½ teaspoon salt, freshly ground pepper and 3 tablespoons oil. Mix well. In another bowl beat 2 egg yolks with 120ml/4fl oz of water. Add the egg mixture to the flour along with 1½ teaspoons baking power. Knead until you have a smooth dough. Roll the dough on a floured board as thin as you can. Cut into squares 3-inches wide. Cut the leftover meat into small cubes. You need about 300g/11oz of ground meat. Add enough pan juices to moisten the meat. Then add 1 onion finely chopped and mix well. Correct the seasoning, adding salt and pepper if necessary. Place 1 teaspoon of the ground meat in the centre of the square. Moisten the edges with water and fold the dough to form a triangle; press the dough down to seal the meat. Repeat this step until all the meat has been used.

In a saucepan bring 3.5 litres/6 pints of water to a boil. Add the kreplach and bring to a boil, lower the heat to medium. Cook until the kreplach rise to the top. Remove with a slotted spoon and add to a strong chicken soup.

Pork with Chinese Chestnuts and Chinese Celery

Chinese chestnuts are small and round and can be bought at any Asian store, or you can use preserved chestnuts. Chinese celery has very thin stalks and is full of flavour. Normal celery can also be used here. Ask your butcher to cut in thin slivers 450g/1lb of pork from the leg. Peel 3 garlic cloves and coarsely chop. Cut off the celery leaves (use to make soup) and thinly chop 4 stalks. In a large skillet heat 1 tablespoon oil. When the oil is hot add the pork and quickly sauté over high heat along with the garlic. Add ½ tablespoon of sesame oil, the chestnuts and the celery. Sauté for 4 minutes. Add salt and pepper to taste. Sprinkle with 2 tablespoons of chopped coriander and serve with steamed rice. Serves 4.

Juliette's Chocolate Truffles

In a food processor place 2 tablespoons unsweetened cocoa, 2 tablespoons brandy, 40g/1½ oz walnuts, 4 tablespoons butter cut into small pieces, 450g/1lb confectioner's icing sugar, 2 tablespoons corn syrup, 1 tablespoon double cream and a pinch of salt. Process all the ingredients until the mixture is a thick paste. Remove to a bowl. Wet your hands slightly and roll the cocoa mixture between the palms of your hands into small balls about 1-inch in diameter. Place 40g/1½ oz nuts (almonds, pecans or hazelnuts) in a food processor and process until chopped fine. Transfer the chopped nuts into a bowl. In another bowl place 120g/4oz of cocoa. Roll the balls first in the chopped nuts, then in the cocoa. Place the truffles in a sealed container and refrigerate for 24 hours. Yields about 30 truffles.

Also available in ISIS Large Print:

Return to Paris

Colette Rossant

In Apricots on the Nile, Colette Rossant's bestselling memoir, we left her as a fifteen-year-old sailing away from her beloved Cairo to her mothers family in France. It is 1947 and Paris is recoving from the war. As soon as they arrive, Colette's mother abandons her yet again, leaving her with her grandmother. Lonely, frightened and homesick, Colette finds solace in the kitchen with the cook, Georgette, and discovers a love for French food. And it is through food that Colette finally finds happiness in Paris, skipping school to visit farmers' markets in Port de Neuilly and dining in famous restaurants with her new stepfather, a hotelier who shares her love of eating. Then at sixteen, upon meeting a dashing young American holidaying in Paris, she makes up her mind and never looks back.

ISBN 978-0-7531-9882-7 (hb)
ISBN 978-0-7531-9883-4 (pb)

Apricots on the Nile:
A Memoir with Recipes

Colette Rossant

In 1937, five-year-old Colette Rossant arrived in Cairo from Paris with her Egyptian-Jewish father and beautiful French mother. When her father dies Colette's flighty mother abandons the little girl to her wealthy grandparents. She soon settles into their luxuriant, food-centered lifestyle — spending afternoons in the spice-filled kitchen; accompanying her grandmother to the bazaar and feasting on the delicious food. At fifteen Colette is brought back to Paris with her mother, never to see her grandparents again, and only to return to Egypt thirty years later. In this charming, funny, and moving memoir, accompanied by mouth-watering recipes, she evokes an Egypt lost, to her and to us, for ever.

ISBN 978-0-7531-9880-3 (hb)
ISBN 978-0-7531-9881-0 (pb)

ISIS publish a wide range of books in large print, from fiction to biography. Any suggestions for books you would like to see in large print or audio are always welcome. Please send to the Editorial Department at:

ISIS Publishing Limited
7 Centremead
Osney Mead
Oxford OX2 0ES

A full list of titles is available free of charge from:

Ulverscroft Large Print Books Limited

(UK)
The Green
Bradgate Road, Anstey
Leicester LE7 7FU
Tel: (0116) 236 4325

(Australia)
P.O. Box 314
St Leonards
NSW 1590
Tel: (02) 9436 2622

(USA)
P.O. Box 1230
West Seneca
N.Y. 14224-1230
Tel: (716) 674 4270

(Canada)
P.O. Box 80038
Burlington
Ontario L7L 6B1
Tel: (905) 637 8734

(New Zealand)
P.O. Box 456
Feilding
Tel: (06) 323 6828

Details of **ISIS** complete and unabridged audio books are also available from these offices. Alternatively, contact your local library for details of their collection of **ISIS** large print and unabridged audio books.